VILÉM FLUSSER

Electronic Mediations

**Katherine Hayles, Mark Poster,
and Samuel Weber, Series Editors**

(continued on page 178)

Vilém Flusser

An Introduction

Anke Finger, Rainer Guldin,
and Gustavo Bernardo

Electronic Mediations

VOLUME 34

University of Minnesota Press
MINNEAPOLIS
LONDON

Portions of this book were previously published in Portuguese as *Vilém Flusser: uma introdução* (São Paulo, Brazil: Annablume Editora, 2008) and in German as *Vilém Flusser* (Munich, Germany: UTB/Fink, 2009). Portions of chapter 7 were previously published as "Idea/Imagination/Dialogue: The Total Artwork and Conceptual Art," in *The Aesthetics of the Total Artwork: On Borders and Fragments,* ed. Danielle Follett and Anke Finger (Baltimore: The Johns Hopkins University Press, 2011).

Photographs courtesy of Dinah and Edith Flusser.

Published by the University of Minnesota Press
111 Third Avenue South, Suite 290
Minneapolis, MN 55401-2520
http://www.upress.umn.edu

Library of Congress Cataloging-in-Publication Data

Finger, Anke K.
    Vilém Flusser : an introduction / Anke Finger, Rainer Guldin, and Gustavo Bernardo.
        p. cm. — (Electronic mediations ; v. 34)
        Includes bibliographical references and index.
        ISBN 978-0-8166-7478-7 (hc : alk. paper) — ISBN 978-0-8166-7479-4 (pb : alk. paper)
    1. Flusser, Vilém, 1920–1991. 2. Philosophers—Brazil. I. Guldin, Rainer. II. Bernardo, Gustavo. III. Title.
        B1044.F574F56 2011
        193—dc22

                        2010033910

Printed in the United States of America on acid-free paper

The University of Minnesota is an equal-opportunity educator and employer.

17 16 15 14 13 12 11   10 9 8 7 6 5 4 3 2 1

To Edith Flusser

Die Erste Elegie
Wer, wenn ich schriee, hörte mich denn aus der Engel
Ordnungen? und gesetzt selbst, es nähme
einer mich plötzlich ans Herz: ich verginge von seinem
stärkeren Dasein. Denn das Schöne ist nichts
als des Schrecklichen Anfang, den wir noch grade ertragen,
und wir bewundern es so, weil es gelassen verschmäht,
uns zu zerstören. Ein jeder Engel ist schrecklich.
—Ranier Maria Rilke, *Duineser Elegien*

The First Elegy
Who, if I cried out, would hear me among the Angelic
Orders? And even if one were to suddenly
take me to its heart, I would vanish into its
stronger existence. For beauty is nothing but
the beginning of terror, that we are still able to bear,
and we revere it so, because it calmly disdains
to destroy us. Every Angel is terror.
—Ranier Maria Rilke, *Duino Elegies*

Contents

Acknowledgments

During this last stage of guiding our introduction to Vilém Flusser around the globe to its third continent, my work on this English-language edition has benefited from the help of several generous colleagues and institutions. Many thanks are due to the University of Connecticut Humanities Institute, where parts of the volume were first composed in English (to be then translated into Portuguese and self-translated into German, in Flusserian fashion). Additional research for chapter 7 was greatly facilitated by a grant from the University of Connecticut Research Foundation in 2009. This last chapter also improved significantly under the expert guidance of Nancy Ann Roth. The Flusser Archive located at the University of the Arts in Berlin, Germany (in particular, Marcel Marburger), kindly forwarded important materials when they were needed. Julie Anderson was most attentive to details of language and comprehensibility, obliging me by keeping a general reader in mind. Special thanks go to Holly Monteith and David Fideler for their meticulous copyediting and design. Last, I thank my coauthors, Gustavo Bernardo and Rainer Guldin, who have become trusted friends and colleagues in this most rewarding endeavor to introduce and help explain Flusser's ideas.

— Anke Finger
Storrs, Connecticut, spring 2011

Abbreviations

BO = *Bodenlos: eine philosophische Autobiographie* [Rootless: A Philosophical Autobiography]
DR = *Da religiosidade* [Of Religiosity]
FL = *Filosofia da linguagem* [Philosophy of Language]
FM = *The Freedom of the Migrant: Objections to Nationalism*
GE = *Gesten: Versuch einer Phänomenologie* [Gestures: Attempt toward a Phenomenology]
JS = *Jude sein: Essays, Briefe, Fiktionen* [Being Jewish: Essays, Letters, Fictions]
KO = *Kommunikologie* [Communicology]
LO = *Lob der Oberflächlichkeit: für eine Phänomenologie der Medien* [In Praise of Superficiality: Toward a Phenomenology of Media]
LR = *Língua e realidade* [Language and Reality]
PH = *Pós-História: vinte instantâneos e um modo de usar* [Posthistory: A Corrected Historiography]
PP = *Toward a Philosophy of Photography*
VA = *Vampyroteuthis infernalis: eine Abhandlung samt Befund des Institut Scientifique de Recherche Paranaturaliste* [*Vampyroteuthis infernalis*: A Treatise, Including a Report, from the Scientific Institute for Paranaturalist Research]
VZ = *Vom Zweifel* [On Doubt]
WF = *Does Writing Have a Future?*
ZG = *Zwiegespräche: Interviews 1967–1991* [Interviews]

Introduction:
Vilém Flusser's Atlases

In a short text titled "My Atlas," Vilém Flusser recounts conversations with a fictitious grandfather, a writer, concerning this grandfather's treasured atlases: "The first atlas served him to localize an event he wanted to describe. The second served to acquire an overview of all the events. In that sense, and thanks to these two atlases, he could simultaneously dive into the world and surface again." But a crisis of orientation ensued, creating a plethora of atlases: they began to explode into different directions at the end of the twentieth century. The resulting and overwhelming variety undermined the atlases' very purpose of providing reliable direction because, according to Flusser, they exploded "in different directions at the same time: in one they obtained colors . . . in another the atlases began to zoom. . . . A third direction of this explosion was the covering of one map with another. . . . In yet another direction history exploded into geography and there were historical atlases." This crisis presented a considerable challenge for the grandfather: "He leafed through these atlases and he noticed how history could be skimmed (blätterbar) rather than continue to flow. History now looked like a badly projected film: Events began to disintegrate in that scenes suddenly leaped."[1] For the grandfather, this new, colorful landscape of atlases became an imaginative play with history, but it also plunged him into abysmal chaos. In the end, to find his bearings within all these wonderful but confusing possibilities of mapping the world and its history, he purposefully returned to his own old and outdated atlases in search of meaning and balance.

Prague and European modernism in their urban expressions presented a first atlas for the young Vilém Flusser—Prague was the center of his world, his gauge for geopolitical and sociohistorical dimensions and his instrument for learning languages and their cultures. Flusser and his family experienced Prague at a time when not only the city and the first Czech Republic took new shapes; central and Western Europe, too, coexisted within constellations that stood for redefined borders and new beginnings among the destruction and turmoil following World War I. There was a new world, a new atlas, surrounding this new republic. Not one envisioned by the Germans; one that, in 1919, brought forth the League of Nations and that began to challenge the power structures between colonial powers and colonies, between empires and vassal countries. At the time of Flusser's birth, on May 12, 1920, the republic was barely one and a half years old. The new president, Thomas G. Masaryk, had embarked on his transatlantic journey from New York to London, moved on to France and Italy, and declared on December 22, 1918, in Prague, as documented in his autobiography from 1927, *Die Weltrevolution,* "We have built our state." For the young Flusser, Prague was home; it was multiplicity, it was inclusion, it was borderless in its wholeness, it was Flusser's introduction to modernity and modernism. But Prague, so soon, turned into the opposite of home: it was division, exclusion, it was an introduction to fascist modernity and modernism; Prague fell apart. The literal and metaphorical border crossings Flusser was forced to experience beginning in 1939 are closely inter-twined with his realization that this seemingly intact universe of Prague, this artwork of the past, would never reemerge as one. In Flusser's mind and memory, this home became incomplete and fragmented.

Flusser's entire oeuvre mirrors such fragmentation: his biography, his books, and his essays are marked by incompletion and border crossings. And although the texts as a whole create the network of his ideas, we should also read them as fragments in the modern sense: as piecemeal, as a constant endeavor, and as his occasionally desperate resistance to boundaries, totality, and totalitarianism. For Flusser never returned to his old atlases, like his fictitious grandfather; he plunged with fervor into the new, colorful landscape of atlases to engage fully in the imaginative play with history and ideas precisely because he, ultimately, embraced the abyss of chaos. Certainly his entire work, though marked by doubt and doom throughout, bespeaks an optimism that accentuates possibility and creativity.

Introducing Flusser

This is the first English-language introduction to Vilém Flusser (1920–91). Though other collections of his texts, most notably *The Shape of Things: A Philosophy of Design,* edited by Martin Pawley (1999); *Writings,* edited by Andreas Ströhl (2002); and *The Freedom of the Migrant: Objections to Nationalism,* edited by Anke Finger (2003),[2] initiated some discussion of Flusser in the English-speaking world, Flusser's philosophy remains practically unknown beyond small circles in German studies, media theory, and digital art. One of these days, we may be able to trace the patterns of international reception histories, and Flusser's will most certainly present itself as complicated: as a Prague Jew, he was forced into exile in 1939, just as he had begun his studies at the renowned Charles University. In his twenties, he was required to work rather than study and establish a reputation as a scholar in the country that provided his visa, Brazil, and he had to learn a new language, Portuguese, to communicate. By the 1970s, the desire—never realized—was to continue an increasingly successful career as a Brazilian philosopher of communication in the United States; instead, he and his wife, Edith Flusser, moved to France. This prolific period and good connections in Europe resulted in fame and almost celebrity status in Germany in the last decades of his life. As a thinker in exile, a migrant, and a polyglot, Flusser wrote and published in four languages, repeatedly translating his own texts, often altering them in the process, and preferring the essay genre. Given his multilingual approach to thinking and writing and, therefore, addressing a selective readership, depending on the language in which a text was published, until recently, Flusser was known only in parts: in Brazil, for his texts on art, language, and communication in Portuguese; in Germany, for his ideas on media theory, technical images, writing, and history in German; and for a few English- and French-speaking readers, for some of the numerous essays published in their languages in between. Klaus Sander has provided invaluable information on the publication history of Flusser's works in the languages listed, although the text itself still awaits publication (it is available in the Flusser Archive in Berlin). Sander's *Flusser-Quellen: Eine kommentierte Bibliographie Vilém Flussers von 1960–2000,* an annotated bibliography, lists a total of 406 titles in German, 352 titles in Portuguese, 90 titles in English, and 60 in French, among other languages. Many of Flusser's texts, including his letters, remain unpublished and can only be accessed at the archive.

During the first decade of the twenty-first century, however, Flusser scholarship in Brazil, Germany, and the United States has made important adjustments to what heretofore presented itself as a somewhat spotty treatment of Flusser's arguably disjointed texts; key conferences, symposia, and subsequent publications paid closer attention to the philosopher's role within varying linguistic, disciplinary, and national contexts. Subsequent to the important work of Rainer Guldin early in the decade, in 2006, for example, Susanne Klengel and Holger Siever hosted a symposium in Germany that focused on the Brazilian Flusser, resulting in a volume titled *Das Dritte Ufer: Vilém Flusser und Brasilien* (2009).[3] In turn, two conferences, organized by Norval Baitello and Gustavo Bernardo, have taken place in Brazil, taking another look at Flusser's works in general, "ReVer Flusser," and at his idea of fiction, "A Filosofia da Ficção de Vilém Flusser." In 2007, a conference in Prague, organized by Katerina Krtilova, examined Flusser's imprint on philosophy in the Czech Republic, among other topics. A first U.S. conference is still to take place. Perhaps most significantly, Flusser's archive in Berlin, directed by Siegfried Zielinski; the online journal *Flusser Studies*; and a number of engaged and interconnected Flusser scholars have helped bring academics, artists, and general readers from around the world more closely together in person and via publications to investigate Flusser's writings and to exchange information—a dialogue among different languages and cultures Flusser himself would have appreciated.

Significant Texts

The authors of this volume originally intended to create a grid or multilevel visualization of how Flusser's texts and concepts interact with and refer to each other, but despite different attempts, this project failed. Not only does Flusser's multilingual style of writing prevent such a solidification of one text in relation to others, but it also would undermine each text's potential multireferentiality and disciplinary or interdisciplinary interpretations. Instead, we decided to offer short summaries of his most significant works and point to research areas within which they may be of interest. The works are listed following their chronology of publication.

Language and Reality

Language and Reality is the first book by Vilém Flusser, published in Portuguese in 1963 as *Língua e realidade*.[4] The work formulates the following axioms: language is reality; language gives form to reality; language creates reality; language disseminates reality. These axioms generate the question, if language is reality, what would have created language? Flusser's answer is that poetry creates language. Flusser asserts that the universe, knowledge, truth, and reality are linguistic aspects. Taking his cue from Shakespeare, he posits that "the world is but a word." What emerges through the senses and what we call "reality" is raw data that become real only within the context of language, the only instance that creates reality. However, as languages are plural and differ in their structure, the realities created by them also vary.

The History of the Devil

The History of the Devil was published in Portuguese in 1965 as *A história do diabo*.[5] It is a masterpiece of irony and philosophy. Flusser studies the devil from the perspective of the seven deadly sins: Pride, Greed, Lust, Envy, Gluttony, Anger, and Laziness. But his irony subverts the definition of each sin. Pride represents the consciousness of the self and takes place in the arts. Greed forms the basis of the economy. Lust represents instinct and therefore affirms life. Gluttony compels humans to fight for improving life by means of technology. Envy compels humans to fight for social justice and political freedom. Anger assures the denial of restrictions to our will, lending dignity to humans and leading us to engage in science. Laziness, or sadness, is the highest stage, reached by quiet meditation or philosophy. In other words, as Flusser would put it, the devil is the real creator of our civilization.

Posthistory

Posthistory was published first in Portuguese in 1983 as *Pós-história*.[6] According to Flusser, the event "Auschwitz" establishes our posthistory. Auschwitz represents the reification of the human being into an object. History, therefore, is a concept that implies the notions of linearity and progress. However, the models that inform our society today are no longer linear. Posthistory, rather, comes in the form of apparatuses that program us and in the form of barbarians who want to destroy the apparatuses; but these barbarians do not realize that the impulse of destruction is part of that programming. One does not fight against progress by calling oneself "progressionist." One fights against progress by slowing progress—or by leaving the anonymous mass to take care of the loneliness of a lighthouse.

Toward a Philosophy of Photography, Into the Universe of Technical Images, and Does Writing Have a Future?

These three texts stand on their own, but they also form a trilogy, building on each other, and as such present the core of Flusser's media theory. Published in German in 1983, 1985, and 1987, respectively, the first text[7] sets the stage for Flusser's theory of the technical image, beginning with what he refers to as posthistory: the beginnings of the photographic image conclude the teleology of writing, and history comes to an end. Widely acknowledged as one of the most original texts on photography, and comparable in significance to the studies by Walter Benjamin, Roland Barthes, Susan Sontag, and others, Flusser discovers the photograph as a technical image and interprets it as a "metacode of texts" rather than as a mimetic image aiming for objectivity. This small book remains one of Flusser's most influential and successful publications. In *Into the Universe of Technical Images*, Flusser develops his five-step model of cultural history at the end of which we find the technical images.[8] Images cannot be compared anymore to traditional depictions or visual creations; they have become flat, they disintegrated into pixels and became grainy, forcing us to gather them and make them compact. As a result, calculating and computing, according to Flusser, marks what he calls a "cultural revolution," a new era of completely different media. Finally, *Does Writing Have a Future?* addresses Flusser's concern with the cultural change from writing as an instrument to inscribe the teleology of human history to the era of technical images in which circularity rather than progress characterizes humans' sense of being-in-the-world and communication.[9] Slowly, by analyzing, for example, letters as images and by picking apart images to recognize them as texts, we are moving from the alphanumerical code into a digital one; what may prevent us from discovering a whole new experience and practice of reading and communicating and from employing creative powers heretofore unknown to us are the limits of our categories of thought. Reexamining "culturemes" such as letters also requires us to reexamine the categories to which we have become accustomed. Chapter 5 of this volume discusses Flusser's media theory in greater detail.

Vampyrotheutis infernalis

Published in German in 1987 with the subtitle *A Treatise, Including a Report, from the Scientific Institute for Paranaturalist Research*, this fable about a certain species of cephalopods could easily serve as Flusser's contribution to animal or posthuman studies.[10] The book was coauthored with Louis Bec, a close friend of the Flussers in

France and an artist interested in imagining new zoomorphic creatures, thereby interlocking art and science. Flusser and Bec here treat the *Vampyroteuthis infernalis* as an antipode to humans and establish a new dialogic or intercultural exercise by critiquing anthropocentrism: we humans eventually observe ourselves by passing through and learning about the world, behavior, and mentality of this small creature that literally lives in a universe opposite to ours.

Supposed: A Succession of Scenes

Angenommen: eine Szenenfolge was published in 1989 and presents twenty-two semiautobiographical, fictitious vignettes Flusser termed "scenarios of the future."[11] Philosophizing about three sets of different possibilities, categorized as "Scenes from Family Life," "Scenes from Economic Life," and "Scenes from Politics," the author explicitly suggests ("Wanted!") at the outset to dare to recode the written scenarios as video images, that is, to turn the text into a film or a set of films. As such, *Supposed* may well be considered Flusser's only film script.

Gestures: Attempt toward a Phenomenology

Gestures was first published in 1991 in German as *Gesten: Versuch einer Phänomenologie*.[12] Apart from two introductory chapters and a final theoretical consideration of a possible, all-encompassing interdisciplinary theory of gestures, it contains sixteen phenomenological descriptions of different fundamental human gestures. Flusser offers a wide spectrum that ranges from gestures of writing, filming, videotaping, and photographing to the gestures of pipe smoking and shaving, including gestures of telephoning, listening to music, planting, searching, and doing. Gestures are not just reflexes; they articulate a moment of freedom and are in this sense not fully explicable in causal terms.

Rootless: A Philosophical Autobiography

Bodenlos: eine philosophische Autobiographie was first published in 1992 in German.[13] Flusser wrote the text in the early 1970s after returning to Europe from Brazil. The first part of the book retraces Flusser's life from early exile in 1939, marked by a feeling of loss and disorientation, to the liberating discovery of a radically new culture in São Paulo in the 1940s and especially in the 1950s and 1960s. The painful absence of roots turns into a new liberty, and exile opens up a world of possibilities. The second part of the book consists of a series of short portraits of important Brazilian friends who played pivotal roles in Flusser's intellectual biography.

The Shape of Things: A Philosophy of Design

Published in German in 1993, this collection of essays speaks to Flusser's interests in art, design, and creativity, the latter serving as a potential leitmotif for his thinking and writing in general—Flusser was always more interested in poiesis, in making art and realities, than in mimesis.[14] Comparable to *Gestures,* the philosopher here explores possibilities for different approaches to design, including everyday objects such as the typewriter and tools, proposing to read "Design as Theology."

Brazil or the Search for a New Human: Toward a Phenomenology of Underdevelopment

Flusser's *Phenomenology of the Brazilian* was published postmortem in German, in 1994, as *Brasilien oder die Suche nach dem neuen Menschen: Für eine Phämenologie der Unterentwicklung.*[15] It was written in the early 1970s, when Flusser returned to Europe to live in France and when he could see and interpret, once again with the eyes of a foreigner, the country in which he spent thirty years of his life. By using a phenomenological approach, the philosopher tries to realize a Brazilian *epoché*. According to Flusser, the Brazilian is not a state but a process. The Brazilian can be the source of the new man: a new man able to break an internal reification, objectification and alienation.

Being Jewish: Essays, Letters, Fictions

Jude sein: Essays, Briefe, Fiktionen, was first published in German in 1994.[16] The book, a compilation of essays, letters, and reminiscences, presents perhaps his other most autobiographical text, concentrating on Flusser's identity as a Jew from existential, cultural, and religious perspectives. Flusser hardly considered himself a Jewish thinker, but especially in his theory on history and historiography, in his later writings, and in his exchanges with his cousin David Flusser, a well-known scholar of early Christianity and Judaism and an orthodox Jew, he eagerly debated what it means to be Jewish: "to be there for the other." In existential terms, and by critiquing Sartre, Flusser reads being Jewish as follows:

> When others look at me as a Jew (and the others are not just anti-Semites, but particularly my own family), then I recognize myself in this gaze and likewise view them with a Jewish gaze. Hence it is true that I am only what I am by this function of another gazing at me; this does not mean, however, that I am not what I "really" am. Although I am only theoretically a Jew, I am nonetheless a Jew. Put differently: I am only what I am, including being Jewish, within the categories that others attach to me (intersubjectivity); and without these categories, in isolation, I am, strictly speaking, nothing. I do not exist without the gaze of the other. (*JS,* 65)

From Subject to Project: On Becoming Human

From Subject to Project was first published posthumously in 1994 in German as *Vom Subjekt zum Projekt: Menschwerdung.*[17] This volume contains Flusser's very last writings. The central notion is the opposition of subject and project. According to Flusser, human beings should become active projectors of possible lives lived and alternative worlds created. The second part, *Menschwerdung* (becoming human), is incomplete, as Flusser died before being able to finish it. In *Menschwerdung,* Flusser reconstructs the anthropological past of the human species from a phenomenological point of view. This text not only serves as a summary of Flusser's late philosophy but also sparkles as a highly poetical piece of writing, brimming with wordplay and innovative imagery.

Communicology

Communicology was first published posthumously in 1996 in German as *Kommunikologie.*[18] It contains two series of lectures held by Flusser in the 1970s in France: "Lectures on Communicology" (1976–77) and "Mutation in Human Relations?" (1977–78). The latter text is the most exhaustive compendium of Flusser's communication theory before his theoretical shift in the early 1980s. It addresses his notions of dialogue and discourse, the relationship of texts and images, and the initial concepts of technical images and the technical imagination. Flusser also describes a series of discursive and dialogical communication structures: theater, pyramid, tree, amphitheater, circle, and net.

Flusser, Interdisciplinarily

The books listed previously speak to a number of fields, most obviously Continental philosophy. Flusser did consider himself first and foremost a philosopher. Yet Flusser's texts have appealed, and will continue to appeal, to a growing number of readers whose interests emerge from one or more fields, and we are pointing to just a few of them to tie Flusser's oeuvre into established, current, or emerging discussions within and beyond academia.

Most significantly, and at the beginning of the twenty-first century, Flusser no longer just speaks to those euphoric about new media and possible virtual realities, so dominant in media theory in the early and mid-1990s. With his interconnected ideas about the archiving, storage, and distribution of information, memory, communication, and dialogue, Flusser today addresses just as much the scholar of digital culture or media anthropology and archaeology, the librarian intrigued by new methodologies and technologies in the digital humanities, or the general reader trying to keep pace with everyday technical tools, working to understand how we interact with them and how they may influence or change us. The reemerging interest in phenomenology, with two new monographs on Edmund Husserl by Dermot Moran and David Woodruff Smith,[19] and many other interdisciplinary studies that employ a phenomenological approach, places Flusser within an important lineage of practicing phenomenologists in the twentieth century, among them not just Heidegger and Merleau-Ponty but also Gustav Shpet and Jan Patočka. Flusser's focus in *Gestures,* in his texts on language and communication and in his considerations of art, science, and creativity, is nourished by his interest in Husserl, certainly one of his major influences.

Readers engaged in animal studies, too, may find Flusser's texts of interest, certainly his fable about the *Vampyroteuthis,* as he scrutinizes therein what Matthew Calarco has called "the metaphysics of subjectivity": "The subject is not just the *fundamentum inconcussum* of modernity but is the avowedly human locus of this foundation—and this point needs to be explicitly recognized and contested as such."[20] Flusser would agree. His case study in marine and cephalopods' adventures would consequently also fit well into the catalog of *Animal Lessons: How They Teach Us to Be Human,* discussed by Kelly Oliver, and adds to the pedagogies of Rousseau, Derrida, De Beauvoir, Lacan, and Agamben, among others.[21] More significantly, perhaps, studies of the posthuman, including the latest thread of discussions initiated by Katherine Hayles in 1999, may integrate Flusser's work on apparatuses, the technical image, codes, communication, and most important, the human as project in *From Subject to Project,* a negative anthropology.[22]

Migration studies and inter- or transcultural studies present another set of interdisciplinary fields where Flusser's work, significantly his collection on *The Freedom of the Migrant: Objections to Nationalism* and his writings on language and nomadism, opens new venues for debate. In his essay "The Challenge of the Migrant," for example, he sets out to view migration and loss of one's homeland from a unique perspective:

> Homeland is not an eternal value, but rather a function of a specific technology; still, whoever loses it suffers. This is because we are attached to heimat by many bonds, most of which are hidden and not accessible to consciousness. Whenever these attachments tear or are torn asunder, the individual experiences this painfully, almost as a surgical invasion of his most intimate person. When I was forced to leave Prague (or got up the courage to flee) I felt that the universe was crumbling. I fell into the error of confusing my private self with the outside world. It was only after I realized, painfully, that these now severed attachments had bound me that I was overcome by that strange dizziness of liberation and freedom, which everywhere characterizes the free spirit. I first experienced this sense of freedom in

London, in that country that strikes many continentals as almost Chinese, at the beginning of the war, during a time of foreboding about the coming human horror in the camps. The transformation of the question "Free from what?" to "Free for what?"—an inversion that is characteristic of freedom gained—has since accompanied me like a basso continuo on my migrations. All of us nomads who have emerged from it share in the collapse of settledness.[23]

Flusser's objections to nationalism here do not originate from a political or post- or supranational position; the "collapse of settledness" describes both a physical and intellectual necessity and the preparedness to acknowledge encrusted forms of existence to break through them and leave them behind. Cutting the knots metaphorically, as painful as that may be, allows for exploration in new fields of thought and action, a kind of process model against stagnation and lethargy: "Patriotism is symptomatic of a diseased aesthetic. . . . A home is the foundation of all consciousness because it permits us to perceive the world. But dwelling is also anesthetizing because it itself is not perceived but only dimly sensed. This internal contradiction becomes even clearer when one confuses dwelling with heimat and the primary with the secondary. Because the settled person is so enmeshed in his heimat it requires a conscious effort to perceive the world out there."[24]

About This Book

Flusser spent his entire life perceiving, traveling, and examining the world, and this volume presents an attempt at bringing his thoughts and writings to that which he observed—into the world. The chapters each focus on a particular issue in Flusser's philosophy and writings, seeking to highlight significant elements of his fluctuating and cross-referential almost-system of thought. Chapter 1 provides a short summary of his biography, linking his life to the essay genre, Flusser's preferred instrument of thought and composition. Chapter 2 highlights a significant point of departure for his ideas, the thorny question of doubt. Chapter 3 focuses on his lifelong practice of multilingualism and translation, both elements of his everyday life that he sought to translate into the phenomenological and intercultural, intersubjective aspects of his philosophy as well. Chapter 4 endeavors to widen the notion of Flusser as philosopher of communication and as media theorist to include his indebtedness to Husserl and cultural critique in general. Chapter 5 examines his ideas on communication and media theory, and chapter 6 continues by branching out into adjacent fields of science, fiction, and calling attention to Flusser's adamant effort to close the gap between the natural sciences and the humanities by advocating what Don Ihde has referred to as *Expanding Hermeneutics*.[25] Chapter 7, finally, connects Flusser with the art world and concludes the introduction by discussing a fundamental term at the core of his philosophy: *creativity*.

Though each chapter is the product of one of the authors listed here, each editor has contaminated and influenced the entire text based on his or her ideas, interpretation, and style of composition—within limits, of course. This book, therefore, just as much as the Brazilian edition (assembled and supervised by Gustavo Bernardo) and the German (assembled and supervised by Rainer Guldin), displays its own marks left by the editor, in this case, Anke Finger (and all remaining errors are her own). After all, the grandfather's atlases inspired us as well: we wish to make some of Flusser's philosophical atlases available to the general reader, but there remains much territory to be discovered and mapped.

1 | Migration, Nomadism, Networks: A Biography

In a 1991 interview with Patrick Tschudin in Robion, France, Vilém Flusser defined *biography* not as the chronology of a life but as a list of networks: "A biography cannot be about some sort of 'I.' And it seems to me that anyone who tries to describe his own life history has never lived. Rather, I think that a biography consists of the listing of networks through which a current of experiences was run" (*FM*, 89). Although a list of networks does not necessarily exclude the notion of chronology, one network followed by another, Flusser rejected the belief that throughout our life stages, we might always be able to connect with some past version of ourselves. What makes us assume that we can link our aged selves to the baby or toddler who crawled on its mother's lap? Flusser, for one, did not "think that there is any relationship between the I who is talking to you now, who is linked to you . . . and the little brat from Prague" (*FM*, 89). In this first chapter, we will attempt to list some of the many networks within which Flusser found himself or within which—later in life—he chose to operate and live. They shall serve to present a certain chronology, and they are themselves an expression of Flusser's life as continuous and simultaneous essays, his preferred genre of putting his thoughts into writing, as well as expressions of his identity as a migrant and nomad, biographically as well as intellectually. However, as networks, they include voices other than his own, most especially that of his wife, Edith Flusser, née Barth, whose interviews we occasionally cite here.[1]

The networks themselves can be assembled in four clusters or cycles Flusser himself set up in the German version of his autobiography *Bodenlos*: "monologues, dialogues, discourses, and reflections." In the French version, Flusser categorized his life's networks in slightly different terms: "Passivité. Disponibilité. Engagement. Dégagement." Rainer Guldin, who has called attention to the difference between these two versions, recognizes that those cycles carry both chronologic and synchronic meaning for Flusser: "In both versions the four parts represent not so much different phases of life to be passed through successively; rather, they signify an equal amount of specific possibilities to encounter the world; they are intertwined possibilities within a complex network of relations."[2] This chapter will present to the reader the chronology of Flusser's networks in lieu of a strictly conventional biography; in doing so, we shall weave in aspects of his work that are closely related to his biography, the essay, and the epistemological positions from which he observed the phenomena he encountered, that of the migrant and expellee and, ultimately, the intellectual nomad. Correspondingly, the networks—and the chapter—are structured according to the cities or towns that facilitated his relations to those close and distant. For cities represented networks to Flusser as well. He viewed them as projects "in which identity and difference . . . give rise to one another." He also valued them as dislodgments of the self:

> The notorious Self is seen as a knot in which different fields cross. . . . The notorious Self shows itself not as a kernel but

as a shell. It holds the scattered parts together, contains them. It is a mask. From this it follows that the city can no longer be a place in which individuals come together but, on the contrary, is a groove in fields where masks are distributed. The self does not come to the city in order to come together with others but, on the contrary, just the opposite. It is first in the city that the self arises as the other of the others.[3]

Prague

Possibilities abounded for Vilém Flusser when he was born on May 12, 1920. His mother, Melitta (née Basch), came from a noble family, and his father, Gustav, was an intellectual and a business-man (the latter by default, thanks to his father-in-law) who had entered politics in Tomáš G. Masaryk's new Czech Republic. The year of Flusser's birth was far from serene, though, as the new republic tried to establish itself as an independent political entity while a plethora of diverse groups fought or coexisted along ethnic, linguistic, or political lines:

> The spring and summer of 1920 were turbulent seasons, and by mid-November the disorders reached Prague again. Once again the national groups had had a difficult time adjusting to each other; in the countryside, Czech soldiers, legionnaires, and Sokols, supported by nationalist journalists, were less than tolerant, and the Germans were unwilling or unable to grasp that they had grievously underestimated the political potential of the Czechs, whom they had been looking down upon for so long.[4]

In 1918, T. G. Masaryk had made sure that Jews were provided full citizenship rights, and in 1919, Prague was home to a Jewish Party. However, there was no homogeneous Jewish community in Prague, and multiple identities, associations, and languages confronted and inspired young Vilém in his first decade as a privileged member of Prague's German- and Czech-speaking Jewish community.

His father, he remembered in a letter to Dr. Joseph Fränkl, published in *Jude sein*, "studied mathematics and physics in Vienna (with Einstein, among others), and, naturally, philosophy as well. . . . This is how he met Tomáš Garrigue Masaryk and became one of those 'Pátecníci' [members of a Friday salon, A.F.] who shaped the CSR so profoundly" (*JS*, 13). Gustav Flusser taught mathematics, translated books by Masaryk into German, became a member of parliament for the social democrats in 1918, and published a recently reissued treatise titled *Deutsche Politiker an das tschechische Volk* [German Politicians to the Czech People] in 1921. By 1924, he had left politics, and at the end of the 1920s, he took on the directorship of the Prague Handelsakademie (commercial academy), where he also taught mathematics.[5]

In the same letter, Vilém Flusser described his mother as a *fille rangée*, a "dutiful daughter," who was married off in 1919 to a man twelve years her senior to secure the family fortune:

> One can imagine the scandal, a leftist intellectual marries Miss Basch and refuses to give up his ideas, despite the fact that my grandfather Basch immediately made my father a "quiet partner" of his factory. . . . I think that was the silent tragedy of my parents' marriage: the haughty "thinker" and the much younger, cultivated, and reserved "fille rangée." But I think, too, that it was a good marriage: my father "educated" my mother, and she "cultivated" my father. (*JS*, 16)

In short, the families Basch and Flusser, grandparents, parents, and Flusser's sister Ludovika, who was born in December 1922, shared a prosperous and prominent existence on Bubenecska 5 in Dejvice, at least in Vilém's memories: "We led . . . a bourgeois life in the Bubencer house and in the country house my father bought on the estuary of the Moldau" (*JS*, 17).

When Vilém attended the German Realgymnasium in Smíchov, he met Edith Barth. Both lived on the same street, Edith in a house that had been built by a relative of her mother's, the well-known architect Viktor Fürth. It was a large affair with a garden, a pool, servants, and a governess. Her father, Gustav Barth, was a successful businessman who came from a Czech-speaking area in the Bohemian forest, attended school in Plzen, worked in Spain, was a soldier in the war, and opened Koruna, Prague's first fully automated restaurant in the new republic. Her mother, Ernestine (or Anjuschka), came from a German-speaking background in Saatz. Edith was also born in 1920, two months after Vilém, in July. She attended Czech schools at first and resisted speaking German until her parents made her attend the Prague Lyceum. She did not really fit in anywhere, a child from a rich family who was a passionate horsewoman, who went skiing, and who spent afternoons tormenting the governess with her younger sister Eva. At sixteen, and against her parents' wishes—they would rather have seen her study at the university—she enrolled in the Handelsakademie where Gustav Flusser served as director. Her goal was to be able to help her father in business.

At approximately this same time, when they were sixteen or seventeen, Edith noticed Vilém for the first time: "I met my husband when I was seventeen. That was on the hill. On this hill, we lived up there, and he did, too. And in order to get to the city you needed to walk down this hill. And we went down, he, his father, and his sister Ludovika."[6] They also attended dance school together, something of a disappointment for Edith if she had any interest in Vilém at this point: "My husband was there as well, I knew him already. He only went there on my account, and only to eat because they sold sandwiches there. He went, he ate, and didn't dance."[7] The parents knew each other, the mothers played bridge together, and neither party had any objections to the two youngsters turning into a pair. What brought them together? According to Edith, at first, "my husband was full of disdain, I was too rich; he was very much a leftist. Yes, and the Spanish Civil War brought us together, we discussed it. . . . For some time, we also joined the Zionists and we thought of emigrating to Israel. That was our only political engagement."[8] They spent many an afternoon in parks, Vilém eager to teach Edith: "We went for walks a lot. I always had to learn, my husband always educated me. We walked in the parks, we sat and I had to listen. I always had to learn. And it began with Marxism. . . . I had to know exactly what Marxism was, that was the first lesson I received. I always had to learn, it was his greatest pleasure to teach me."[9] The only regular activity to which Edith did not put an end was horse riding.

Little is known about Flusser's development in school and during his first year at Prague's Univerzita Karlova, where he enrolled in 1938 as a student of law, following his Czech and German Matura (*JS*, 17). He must have been an excellent student if one is to take Edith Flusser at her word. He read voraciously about cultural history and politics, among other subjects, and his teacher at the Realgymnasium credited him with significant talents in philosophy. Enthusiastic about learning from the very beginning, he was eager to share what he read and thought about so that, according to his wife, he soon thought of her as a perpetual audience and turned her into his first student. Together they attended a lecture by Martin Buber, for example, an experience that marked Flusser for the rest of his life. The intellectual and cultural stimulations, in fact, were many at the time, all under the auspices of Masaryk's new Czech Republic:

During the period between the World Wars, Prague was—
to name just a few examples—the center of a new Czech
culture inspired by Masaryk, it was a focal point of European Jewish cultural life, and it was a center of that kind
of German culture in which the tradition of the Habsburg
monarchy blossomed anew. These three cultures pollinated
each other in confrontation and in collaboration to such an
extent that one could detect at the time the beginning of
many of the tendencies at play today. One only needs to
think of the Prague Linguists, of Kafka, of Prague's experimental theater, of phenomenology, of Einstein's lectures at
the university, and of the psychoanalytical experiments. To
grow up in such a climate, to sense these productive tensions
in one's surroundings and within oneself, to participate in
them actively since puberty, was entirely natural for the
son of Jewish intellectuals. Only through the distance of
time and space did this naturalness emerge as a privileged
situation. (*BO*, 14–15)

But the pleasures and promises of a blissful youth came to
an abrupt and unexpected end in March 1939. The Slovaks had
declared independence from the republic on March 14 and had
sided with the Nazis, who promptly invaded the country the
next day. Prague, experienced by Flusser and his future wife,
Edith, as the center of the universe and as a reality that could
not possibly vanish, "crumbled and successively fell into the
abyss in pieces" (*BO*, 23). The events appeared to be downright
outlandish: "Something like this was possible in the Middle
Ages or in central Africa (that is, in areas located outside of
any possibility of experience), but not on the Kärntnerstrasse"
(*BO*, 23). Edith Barth's father had sensed this dramatic turn for
the worst early on and had maneuvered his possessions outside
Prague and into England. Edith had visited London several times

before it was decided that they were all to escape to London to seek a life elsewhere. To this day, she remembers the ferocious fight between her father and her prospective father-in-law, who refused to leave the country: "My father-in-law had received an invitation to the university in Jerusalem, the entire family would have been able to emigrate. And I remember, I see a dispute, a fight, between my father and my father-in-law . . . you must, you must, you must go, you cannot stay here, you have a wife, you have children—and he remained quiet. . . . And that was terrible then. It was like a fight."[10] Gustav Flusser, despite his astuteness, and despite incoming offers to assume positions outside Prague, considered his duties and his loyalties at home, according to the daughter-in-law he never was able to appreciate as such, and he remained in Prague. As Ines Koeltzsch points out in her exceedingly well-researched article, his name could no longer be found among those teaching in summer 1939. He was arrested earlier that year and was taken to Dachau in September, and then to Buchenwald.

His son disagreed with this course of inaction and turned to the Barth family. If Edith were to leave for London, Vilém would follow. The Barths realized that they now had to move to London for good; Edith's father and her sister had already left, but Edith continued to return to Prague because of Vilém. She and her mother had moved out of their house on the hill and found shelter here and there in the city. They possessed precious visas to England, but the Gestapo stipulated that their husband and father return to Prague before they would permit them to depart as well. They were desperate. For several days, they lined up to obtain the necessary Gestapo stamp in their passports, with Edith's mother in a panic. Finally, on the third or fourth day of waiting in line, Edith remembers, they arrived at the desk staffed with a screaming officer and his young assistant. While the officer yelled insults at them, it was the young

Vilém Flusser, São Paolo, Brazil, 1950s

Edith and Vilém Flusser with their sons Victor and Mischa, São
Paulo, Brazil, airport, 1969 or 1970

The Flussers in Marseille, 1980s

The Flussers in Robion with their dog Alma, mid-1980s

Flusser on one of his many travels to West Germany, late 1980s

assistant who saved their lives: he snatched the two passports the officer had slammed on the table and stamped them behind the other's back. Once outside and away from the terror, the two women realized that they were free to go.

Vilém had long ago received his own stamp because, at first, everyone was allowed to emigrate if he had the means. With their stamps in place, the three of them took the train together to the Dutch border on or around March 20, 1939. For Vilém, this departure was agony:

> The decision to escape had immediate and horrendous results. I had died for my parents, siblings, and closest friends, and they had died for me. I looked into their faces and saw death masks. I was a ghost among ghosts. When I, much later and successively, received news of their various and gruesome deaths, it was only an affirmation of that which I had experienced back then. With the decision to escape they had already departed into the realm of shadows, and their murder was only the automatic execution of a process that had taken form back then. Not the Nazis—I myself had murdered them with my decision to escape in order to save my shadowy self. . . . This is how Prague died. (*BO*, 28–29)

At the same time, this excruciating pain carried the seeds of Flusser's sense of liberation; of his perspectives as a person in permanent exile, a migrant, and a nomad; and of his life as a ceaseless essay. These last days in Prague seemed to him nothing but a charade, a puppet theater that could not present a home anymore. He escaped, but he also became *bodenlos*: without territory. He realized, although with a "bleeding heart," that "from now on, everything was possible" (*BO*, 30).

The Dutch border put an abrupt end to their escape. Whereas Edith and her mother had long since obtained visas for England,

Vilém had his departure stamp but no visa—for England or for Holland. This proved the fate of many of the Prague Jews traveling with them on the train, and Flusser was required to stay behind, pondering a dreadful possibility: if he did not acquire a visa within three days, the Dutch would send him back and to a concentration camp. He stayed at the border while Edith, now herself in a panic, went ahead with her mother to London, hoping that her father would be able to help: "I was beside myself, we went to England and the first thing I told my father was that he must, must get my husband out of there, somehow."[11] Flusser was saved. Apparently, Gustav Barth bribed a civil servant at the Foreign Office who was eager to get back to his pregnant wife in the maternity ward. He picked up Vilém on the Continent while all others had to wait. It was "a miracle," according to Edith in 2007.

London

Flusser was now in effect the Barths' third child, and the Barth family stayed in England for about a year. There Flusser embarked on his practice of living *bodenlos,* without territory or connections and roots; indeed, he viewed the inevitable beginning of the war as a crucial test for such a life. His existence oscillated between benign nihilism—everything was of equal importance or none—and playful voyeurism. His surroundings and the people in them, the geopolitical developments and the various participants, all became reduced to meaningless entities or cause for inconsequential amusement. In an interview from 1980, he confessed that during the war, "I always carried around with me a piece of paper divided into two sections—in one section I had listed the reasons for suicide, in the other the reasons against it" (ZG, 24). In daily life, the almost twenty-year-old tried his best to start anew. He rented an apartment with one of Edith's cousins, he wrote jazz lyrics, and he enrolled at the London School of

Economics. Then the bombardment of London started, and Gustav Barth once again moved his family. He rented a small bus, told the chauffeur to drive as far as the full tank would take them, and they and some other Prague families landed in Cornwall somewhere near Exeter.

In Cornwall, all of them lived in an abandoned manor house for months, waiting. According to Edith, the men played chess, and everyone read or went for walks. Vilém cut everyone's hair because he could not enroll at the university in Exeter. Edith herself apprenticed in the maternity ward in a hospital, but work permits were hard to come by. With trepidation, they witnessed the continuous succession of warplanes up ahead. Soon, and attentive to the danger they were still in, the decision was made to leave England as well, and they went in search of visas once again. The possibilities were limited—Shanghai, Panama, Brazil, perhaps some others. Finally, and only after getting baptized by requirement, did they obtain visas for Brazil. Once more, Flusser joined the Barths on the journey to another country, this time on a ship. In 1940, they traveled to the port of South Hampton. Edith remembers, "I will never forget that—the entire seaport was on fire. It was a sea of fire. Somehow we got through and went onto the ship. . . . And then we left [on the *Highland Patriot*, A.F.] together with a cruiser who protected the ship against submarines."[12]

The monthlong journey took its course in utter darkness—the passengers were not permitted to light so much as a cigarette. Nonetheless, Edith Flusser recalls that—in her innocence as a young adult—she enjoyed the voyage: they became close friends with Alex Kafka and others, they politicized, made conversation, and listened to the news. One day, they finally arrived in Rio de Janeiro. Both Edith and Vilém recall the splendor of light that greeted them; Edith named it the "paradise of Rio," and Flusser described the moment as one of hope: "The light at night was probably the most impressive of all. I had not seen a burning light bulb in a year, and that depressed me more than the bombardment. When I saw the illuminated coast of Rio I had the sense of a good life—in contrast to that life in which human beings suffer excruciatingly" (ZG, 24). Hope, however, lasted only for the few moments during the ship's arrival. Flusser had not yet left the vessel when he was called to say Kaddish in a nearby synagogue: the Nazis had murdered his father on June 18, 1940.

São Paulo

In one of his two essays on the essay genre and why he preferred this style for committing ideas to paper, Flusser distinguished between the treatise (the more academic text) and the essay, and he addressed the necessary choice between the two. But choosing the essay presented problems:

> If I decide on the essay, on my style, and on implicating myself in my topic, I run a risk. It is a dialectical risk: that of losing myself in the topic, and that of losing the topic. . . . This is the danger of the essay—but also its beauty. The essay is not merely the articulation of a thought, but of a thought as a point of departure for a committed existence. The essay vibrates with the tension of the fight between thought and life, and between life and death, that Unamuno called "agony." Because of this the essay does not resolve its topic as the treatise does. It does not explain its topic, so in this sense it does not inform its readers. On the contrary, it transforms its topic into an enigma. It implicates itself in the topic and in its reader. This is what makes it attractive.[13]

Although São Paulo, and Brazil, would not count as one essay but as many, embodying both the networks of people and the network of the city of São Paulo, a "committed existence" on Flusser's part proved impossible at first. Suffering from the "agony" of being alive and thinking death, he very likely was depressed, and he certainly remained suicidal for the better part of the 1940s. To "commit" to an existence would have required a commitment to himself and to some form of a new beginning in Brazil—this was simultaneously ridiculous and unbearable. It was Edith and her relatives who attempted to embark on a modest beginning, first in Rio, and then in São Paulo.

Edith's mother had contacted a cousin in Brazil who welcomed these distant relatives on their arrival. They stayed first in a pension in Rio for a few months, before Edith's parents and sister traveled on to the United States in 1941, equipped with visas that had eluded them in Europe. Vilém began looking for work in São Paulo, and eventually, it was decided that they should get married and move to São Paulo for the duration. They married on January 15, 1941, and Edith was soon pregnant with their first child, Dinah. For her, the new beginning turned out to be a struggle with everyday life. "Tremendously spoiled," as she herself readily admitted in 2007, she did not know how to boil water or make eggs or coffee, let alone run a household. In their little apartment above a garage, she asked the neighbors, German-Jewish women, about basic tasks she had to perform while her husband was working in a business world he loathed. They did not know a word of Portuguese on their arrival.

Flusser read constantly, furnished with books by their friend, Alex Bloch, who worked in a bookstore and to whom he wrote long letters about what he had consumed. But during the day, he worked first in a Czech company, then for his wife's uncle. To him, it was a miserable existence. He abhorred the business world, he had no talent for administration, and he was desperately unhappy. Edith often accompanied him on his way to work because she feared that he would kill himself. He was impassive and lost, a "crazy" person who simply could not find his bearings. Dinah cried at night while he hid in his books, and Edith, soon pregnant with their second child, Miguel, was busy with the children and the household. Flusser portrayed the situation in bleak terms in his autobiography: "On the puppet stage of São Paulo one assumed the role of the 'factor that brings progress.' One lived above the times and looked back and down upon the time of Prague and São Paulo with contempt and interest (a strange combination). That meant that one engaged in business during the day and philosophized at night. One pursued both activities with detachment, and both with disgust" (*BO,* 41).

Things improved in the 1950s. Flusser, now a director at STA-BIVOLT, a factory for radios and transistors, never ceased to seek contacts at the university, and first acquaintances turned into friends, most importantly, Vicente Ferreira da Silva and Dora Ferreira da Silva, Milton Vargas, Samson Flexor, and others. Vargas recalled his first meeting with Flusser at the da Silvas's house:

> Vicente, who had introduced Heidegger's philosophy to Brazil, his wife Dora who was already a quite well-known poet, and I were deeply in conversation when someone knocked at the door. It was a peculiar young man, bald already back then, with a sharp nose and impressive glasses. He was completely unknown to us. Confidently, he introduced himself and said that he was looking for people with whom he could exchange ideas. He added that São Paulo was a desert devoid of people and ideas. (*BO,* 279)

The beginnings of a Brazilian network emerged, and Flusser was soon to teach philosophy, to write, and to lead the life of an intellectual. He became affiliated with the University of São

Paulo, and in 1964, he assumed a professorship for communication sciences at the Fundação A. A. Penteado until 1970.

Edith's and Vilém's social lives improved as well. With time, they moved to a house all their own (although not much bigger than their garage apartment, according to Edith) in the Rua Salvador Mendonça, and a big room in the back of the kitchen and their patio turned into a modern-day salon. Flusser was enormously popular as a teacher, and the students and their friends came in hordes to listen to him talk and discuss his ideas. He started to write in Portuguese in the early 1960s, with his first book being titled *Língua e realidade* (1963), a treatise on linguistics. He wrote for newspapers such as the daily *O Estado de São Paulo* and *Folha de São Paulo*, and many of his essays appeared in the journal of Brazil's Institute of Philosophy under Miguel Reale, *Revista Brasileira de Filosofia*. By the mid-1960s, Flusser was a sparkling and renowned personality in the city, with a reputation as an inspiring philosopher and teacher and as a public figure. But doubts began to creep into his daily life, doubts about the military government, about his engagement in Brazil, and about his ability to "dialogue," that is, to live his "essays," to critique, to see himself in the other, to see his "other" in others and to "commit to an existence":

> Those who live in the form of an essay (that is, those who do not just write essays, but for whom life is an essay in order to write essays) know that the question about what to write presents itself only in negative terms. Everything becomes a topic in the universe of the essay, and, consequently, one has to choose in this Embarras de richesses. . . . However, basically, all these topics were nothing but variations of a single one: How can one get engaged in living without territory *[Bodenlosigkeit]*? This is so because one's own life

(the "essay-life") is a variation of a theme, which could be put aphoristically as follows: "How can you believe in 'Bodenlosigkeit'?" (BO, 92)

Flusser had lost the belief in his own engagement with Brazil and this particular network of his life. In an essay titled "The Patio," he identified the military coup in 1964 as a kind of caesura that marked the end of a period of immense enthusiasm—or illusion—on his part and on the part of Brazil's educated youth. After 1964, Brazil's youth turned sober and grim, or they became implicated in the oppression. Flusser acknowledged that given his own relative youth, he had been swept up in this pre-1964 enthusiasm:

> I, too, believed in part that I was witnessing a thrilling process in which the exhausted culture of the West would experience a renaissance under new conditions in Brazil. New music, new art, new poetry, new theater, and new perceptions about the world erupted around me like mushrooms from the ground. . . . [I], too believed . . . that the deficiencies were the maladies of a child and that the horizon promised a future in which the experiments of our time would come to mature. (BO, 210)

After 1964, however, the unique network of Flusser's patio, the modern-day salon he had built to some prominence, reflected the hardship and conflicts of Brazilian intellectuals who rejected the system: "Young people vanished from sight on a daily basis. The fledgling embryo of a new culture, which, as I had to comprehend now, was not at all viable, became dismembered. The scene had changed: reality had broken through" (BO, 212). Flusser, unable to accommodate those youths who were seeking wisdom from him because he himself had felt utterly powerless, tried to approach the situation soberly, perhaps conservatively. In 1966–67, he even accepted a position as cultural attaché of the Foreign Ministry in Europe and the United States. Yet—and at the risk of being designated a traitor—he had to admit defeat.

By the late 1960s, their three children were out of the house, and Dinah was already working abroad as an ambassador. Brazil itself had advanced almost unrecognizably from a sleepy rural country to a major industrial Latin American power. While his resistance to the dictatorship, his disappointment in the "apparatuses" of Brazil, and his realization that the institutions became increasingly technocratic certainly contributed to the Flussers' plans to depart from Brazil, Flusser himself also saw potential for a continuation of his hard-won career in Europe and the United States. It is a desire he probably always carried within himself, and it was not the first time he contemplated leaving Brazil. He wanted to teach, write, and publish elsewhere. Finally, in 1972, he and Edith rented their house to an American and left their country of residence after thirty-two years. This time, their departure was final. They had visited Europe and the United States repeatedly before, in search of diversion but also in search of affiliations and employment, but now, according to Edith, "they were free."

Robion

Robion as a network and as an essay is misleading in several ways: Robion was not, of course, a big city with many masks to put on and many others with whom to engage in dialogue. Even at the beginning of the twenty-first century, the village barely has four thousand inhabitants, and its idyllic setting in the Provençe starkly contrasts with the megalopolis São Paulo. Indeed, there never seemed to be many prospects for essaying or for an essay-life. Nevertheless, the 1970s and 1980s turned out to comprise Flusser's most prolific period, decades during which he composed the majority of his texts. In a 1969 essay titled "In Search of Meaning," he professed that "I still feel within me much to be articulated. An insistent murmur of language not yet ripened in that sweet, heavy, and mysterious fruit called 'the word.' Who knows? I did not even begin to live, and to philosophize, and all I just wrote is no more than an introduction and preface to the theme: in search of meaning."[14] Robion is also misleading because the Flussers actually did not really live there until the 1980s, and they did not spend a lot of time at home, if that is what we may call Robion: they were on the road constantly, with Edith at the wheel (her husband had bad eyesight and could not drive) and with Vilém belting out Mozart arias with great gusto. They lived a life of nomads, a concept that repeatedly arises in Flusser's texts:

> Nomads are people who pursue some goal. . . . Whatever their goal, their wanderings do not come to an end when the goal has been achieved. All goals are way stations; they are situated next to the pathway (Greek *methodos*), and the wandering, taken as a whole, may be seen as an aimless method. In contrast to the back-and-forth rushing of settled people between the private and the political, the wandering of nomads is open-ended. This seemingly aimless wandering may, however, be an error of perspective on the part of the settled. We settled people have worked out the laws regulating our movements, but not those relating to the sweep of wandering—just as we have worked out the laws regulating a falling stone, but not the vagaries of the wind. It may be that the nomadic existence through steppe and across desert may have the same structure as cloud and wind, while the settled

life of back and forth corresponds structurally to summer and winter. Perhaps nomads live meteorologically, and we, astronomically. Or maybe it would be more apt to say that the rhythms of settled life must be expressed by traditional algorithms; that of nomads by fractal ones. (*FM*, 43)

Their new nomadism opened up to the Flussers various new "fields of potentiality," with Robion as one among many. The field of potentiality that brought them to Europe took the form of preparations for the São Paulo Biennale in 1973. While undertaking research for the Biennale in Geneva, Flusser commenced to weave different networks that secured him lectures at the Institut de l'Environment in Paris as early as fall 1972. Important friends and collaborators emerged from the Paris network, among them, most significantly, Abraham Moles, professor of communication theory in Strasburg, and Louis Bec, with whom he worked on *Vampyroteuthis infernalis* (1987), a book that was created with but also partly inspired by Flusser, as Bec has recently revealed. In a letter to Moles, Flusser voiced his early interest in applying the new technologies more imaginatively: "Have you ever thought of using the new communication technologies (not for 'teaching' it to others) [but] to articulate your ideas?"[15]

They first settled in Meran, a spa resort in South Tyrol, and they continued to travel for Flusser to give lectures, to explore the countryside, and to go hiking and for walks. Edith recounts that France, in particular, was a country and culture they had taken little note of before, having preferred to travel to Switzerland or Austria, but they particularly enjoyed exploring those fields of possibilities. Flusser wrote about nature and, on his wife's urging, commenced his autobiography. They now lived in one of the castles on the Loire; it was 1973. The year 1974 was marked by travels to the United States and talks at Columbia University and other institutions, all without further prospects for a position at U.S. institutions. However, by 1975, Flusser had made his way to the Provençe, continuing to lecture—on *Gestures,* among other topics—and not only at the Institut de l'Environment, but also at the Ecole d'Art d'Aix-en-Provençe and, repeatedly, in Brazil as well. Their lives continued in this fashion until 1980, and it was only then that they finally bought their house in Robion and settled in the Provençe to anticipate the rest of their lives in a "dignified manner": "'Dignified' does not represent to us: to be 'honored' by others (that what you call society), but it means: to accomplish something unbound by financial motives, power or fame."[16]

This humble vision of Flusser's remaining decade differed significantly from the reality in the 1980s. Flusser eagerly agreed to ever more lectures and presentations, to interviews, and to writing texts for a plethora of venues. He may not have enriched himself in the process, but he certainly reached some power and more fame as one of the new media theorists who eloquently and creatively stirred the imagination about an impending digital revolution and who, from today's vantage point, appeared almost clairvoyant. In fact, one could argue that in his zeal, he turned from facilitating and taking part in dialogues within his growing networks to facilitating and implementing networks by rousing his audience in monologues. He confronted and criticized and called for co-creation and activism in the digital age. By the mid-1980s, he had reached the zenith of his career: he had written his famous book on photography, translated into many languages; he had composed *Vampyroteuthis* and his books on gestures, posthistory, and communicology, among many other texts; and he had earned his own columns in the U.S. magazine *artforum* and later in *European Photography.* He was a sought-after orator who inspired and occasionally exhausted his audience.

Such was the case at his very last engagement, in the city of

Prague after the fall of Communism. In November 1991, he and Edith followed an invitation from the Goethe Institute, specifically, from Andreas Ströhl, to give a lecture and hold a small seminar. On their way back on November 27, 1991, Flusser was killed in a car accident. His body rests in the New Jewish Cemetery in the city of his birth. Edith Flusser lives today with her daughter Dinah and her grandson Benjamin in New York City. Their older son Miguel lives in Brazil, and Victor, the youngest, lives in France.

2 | On Doubt: The Web of Language

On September 22, 1966, Flusser published a newspaper article in *O Estado de São Paulo* with a rather unusual title: "?" This question mark, one could argue, functions both as an inter-punctuation and as an existential sign; it is as such nothing less than a sign of our times: the question mark has perhaps taken on greater significance than the cross, than hammer and sickle, than the torch of the Statue of Liberty, because it points to the atmosphere that encloses us. It is an atmosphere of suspicion, of exploration, and of doubt.

Vilém Flusser ranks among a few philosophers who have investigated the multifold meanings of the question mark and the atmosphere of all-encompassing doubt in which we live with tremendous tenacity and with some consequence for his own work. His book *A dúvida* [On Doubt], published posthumously in 1999 and only in Portuguese, was written at the beginning of the 1960s. Since 2006, it has become available in German as well. Why did Flusser withhold the text from publication for such a long time? We can only speculate that he considered this particular text to be more radical than his other works. *On Doubt* offers a "Critique of Pure Doubt," in reference to Kant's *Critique of Pure Reason,* to investigate a central point of convergence in Western thought:

> Doubt is a state of thought with multiple meanings. Doubt can present the end of faith, yet it can also lead to new faith. Doubt terminates all certainty. In extreme cases we can view it as "skepticism," as a kind of reversed faith. In small doses doubt stimulates the thinking process, in excessive doses it paralyzes mental agility. Doubt can be a true joy as an intellectual experience, but it can be agony as a moral one. Doubt, just like curiosity, serves as the cradle of research and, as such, the cradle of all systematic thought. In little quantities doubt kills curiosity and puts an end to all knowledge. The starting point of doubt is always a form of faith . . . that precedes doubt. Faith is the original state of the mind *[Geist]*. The naïve, "innocent" mind believes. It is of "good faith." Doubt closes naivité *[sic]* and innocence down. . . . Doubt is absurd. I ask myself: "Why do I doubt?" "Do I really doubt?" These questions probe deeper than the other question: "What do I doubt?" In fact, I doubt the very last step of the Cartesian method, I doubt the authentic doubt of doubt. I doubt the doubt of doubt's authenticity. (*VZ*, 7)

Dubito ergo sum

Flusser's point of departure is René Descartes's philosophy, which he seeks to critique substantially from within. Flusser argued that Descartes made a grave mistake: he doubted doubt as such. His methodical (or hyperbolic) doubt is first of all a paradoxical strategy to put an end to all doubt. However, if one really seeks to put an end to all doubt, then one essentially obstructs the emergence of philosophy and practices nihilism. Flusser, in contrast, demands that we protect doubt and insists that the intellect does not serve as an instrument to control chaos but rather as "a hymn to that which cannot be controlled" (*VZ*, 47).

Descartes has so far undertaken the most radical philosophical discussion on doubt, more radical than that of the ancient skeptics, most notably in *Discourse on the Method* (1637) and *Meditations* (1641). The philosopher doubted his own senses and his own existence. He practiced doubt, too, though ultimately to end such practice and to gain some sense of solid footing with an eventual certainty free of doubt. Descartes's thought processes led to his insisting that something of certainty must exist: that one can doubt something at all. For Descartes, thinking and doubting are one and the same: every thinking about the world immediately implicates that such thinking is subject to doubt.

To best question the Cartesian cogito, Flusser describes the intellect as a field within which thought happens. He mistrusts the implicitly self-assertive certainty of the sentence "I think" because in that moment of thought, the world becomes foreign to us. We doubt it so that we do not have to doubt ourselves. To state "I think therefore I am" means to insert oneself at the origin and as the cause of thought. It would be considerably less arrogant to state that "thoughts form from within me":

> By describing the intellect as a field within which thought happens we move beyond Descartes's statement "I think therefore I am" by at least one step. Our description of the intellect permits us to doubt the statement "I think" and to replace it with "There are thoughts." . . . The intellect as a field within which thought happens makes superfluous the question "What is the intellect?" By "field" I do not mean to say *what* the intellect is, but to put forth a concept that describes *how* something happens. Earth's gravity is not "something" but it is "how" bodies act in relation to the earth. In just the same way, the intellect is how thoughts act.

> The intellect . . . is not being as such. And conversely, there
> are no unconnected thoughts in the intellect. Thoughts have
> to happen in a particular way within the intellect. . . . The
> correct question is "What is a thought?" (*VZ,* 18–19)

The Critique of Cartesian Doubt

Doubt as a method, the basic tool of modern science, is responsible for the most important achievements of our time.
Nonetheless, behind its presupposition lurks the seed of self-
destruction. Just as Descartes had doubted to put an end to
doubt, researchers pose questions and conduct experiments to
advance toward a final comprehensive theory, a total theory,
that would integrate, for example, the fields of astrophysics and
quantum mechanics. Accordingly, researchers conduct research
only to eliminate it eventually. But where does this lead us? For
Flusser, it led to Auschwitz, where humanity had to learn that
it is capable of the worst deeds, and to Hiroshima, where it
learned that it was capable of creating nothingness. Neither of
these catastrophes was some kind of knotting mistake in history's complicated network; they are logical consequences of
Western patterns of thought, that is, of doubt, which, purport-
edly, seeks to remove doubt.

When he doubted everything but himself, Descartes reduced
the world to a temporary hypothesis. While the real world cannot exist, it is impossible for the *I* not to exist. As the Cartesian *I*
increasingly doubts reality, the more it compensates this doubt
by extending trust toward itself, a process of psychological
compensation: trust in the metaphysical solidity of a thinking
I grows in reverse proportion to the loss of trust in reality. This
process is necessary as there exists no satisfying and consistent
definition of the "I." Because it is only autoaccessible, the *I* does
not possess content that would be divisible and therefore ready for

examination. In this sense, the Cartesian *I* functions like a black hole that draws every meaning close and devours it. Linguists, for example, point out that the word *I* is without reference and thus indicates nothingness. Flusser captures this idea in his vision of an *I* suspended over an abyss of nothingness.

Descartes conceived the *I* of his cogito as a thing-in-itself, prematurely provoking the interruption of methodical doubt at a crucial moment. This interruption lends power to modern science and simultaneously presents the end of the road: it lends power because the ground seems solid; the end of the road consists of the fact that the ground, in reality, is nothing but imaginary. Because Descartes doubts just up to a certain point, he promoted a view, a concept of science that does not question itself radically enough.

Protecting Doubt

Doubt requires at least two coexisting and complementary perspectives. In German, for instance, the number 2 is contained within *doubt (Zweifel)*; yet the prerequisite of this basic duality that facilitates an endless plurality is, indeed, faith: the search for truth, set in motion by doubt itself, requires faith in precisely such a truth. This search will lead up to repeated and numerous crossings and bifurcations: it splits into two (or more) possibilities that, again, split into yet more possibilities. The more we inquire and know, the more we know; the more we know, the more doubt we have to tolerate.

For that reason, Flusser considers doubt a polyvalent state of thought (*VZ*, 7). Doubt commences with faith to question it. This putting-into-question destroys faith or replaces it with new faith. Extreme doubt, in turn, results in a kind of inverted faith, that is, in a kind of nihilism, that blocks and paralyzes every intellectual activity and kills curiosity for good. In a way, Descartes's hyperbolic doubt belongs in this vestibule of nihilism. In small doses, however, doubt stimulates thinking and inaugurates the field of research and knowledge. Flusser, in his analysis, stipulates first and foremost to protect just this kind of doubt.

Modern doubt may be traced back to Descartes, but he had little interest in protecting doubt as a possibility or a vehicle for thought. His methodical doubt, rather, presented a kind of trick to manage his own doubt and to arrive at a final certainty, just like politicians subscribe to the idea that there is a war that will ultimately end all wars. Flusser here calls Descartes into question: Flusser regards the ability to doubt an indispensable tool. Although we are repeatedly exposed to the danger of a schizophrenic split when in a state of doubt, without it, thought, science, and philosophy would not exist. Consequently, instead of doubting so as not to, we doubt within the limits of our own doubting.

Yet, if I am because I think, Flusser asks, what do I think, really? I think a flow of thoughts, one thought following others, doubting the preceding ones. This occurs because thoughts are not self-sufficient; rather, they are interdependent and create each other. They thus transform the subject into a flow of doubting thoughts: the subject is a subject only when this flow continues on and does not come to a halt. As Flusser himself points out, thoughts are processes seeking completion in aesthetics and form inasmuch as they pursue satisfaction that we might call meaning. But thoughts are also processes, which generate new thoughts by reproducing themselves ad infinitum. Thinking is

> a process that moves towards its own completion. We can grasp interrupted and unfinished thoughts and view thinking as a process searching for form, a "gestalt"; this is an aesthetic process. . . . And in the second case thinking becomes

an auto-reproductive process, which automatically leads to new thinking. We can distinguish chains of thought within which individual thoughts form their own chains, hooked into each other to form a texture of thoughts. (*VZ*, 20–21)

The flow of thoughts that makes us who we are turns into a whirl, threatening to swallow us when we ask why we doubt at all. Though it is necessary to doubt, we need to acknowledge a limit that is certain if we do not want to fall into a maelstrom.

Modern Western civilization was created on the basis of Cartesian doubt; that is, it rejected reality to save the ego. In this regard, Flusser notes that intellectual progress occasionally results in a loss of reality. At first, we experience progress as liberation and the defeat of prejudices, that is, as an overwhelming experience; beyond it lies an unconscious and unspoken feeling of guilt, however: it is as if we had betrayed the things. According to Flusser, contemporary philosophy evades two borderline experiences—honest hesitancy, on one hand, and generous theoretical opportunism, on the other—leading both to get stuck at the end of the road of their own doubt: "Although an atmosphere of hesitancy and doubt is intellectually more honest than either engagement or fanaticism, both are really attitudes of desperation. Both attest to the loss of faith in the intellect without trying to surpass nihilistic disposition positively" (*VZ*, 12–13).

What Is Thinking?

The question we should ask facing doubt is as follows: what really is thinking? Flusser here prefers not to talk about persons but rather about a plurality of intellectual units. He describes them as fields within which thoughts happen and that, together, form a kind of net or web.

The comprehensive metaphor of the web anticipates the

World Wide Web and reappears in connection with Flusser's concept of a telematic society as a network of intersubjective relationships in his later texts as well (*LO,* 220). Indeed, already in *Filosofia da linguagem,* published in 1966, he portrays the conversation of Western philosophy as a collective, weblike fabric: "The conversation is a fabric made out of sentences that are connected by links called arguments. It is a flowing fabric, expanding constantly. At certain points in the fabric (it would be better to call them moments) the threads of the arguments cross. . . . The conversation consists of these knots that are tied together by arguments. The conversation is the field of the intellect in which thoughts cross. It is the field of dialoguing 'I.' They are an aspect of the conversation" (*FL,* 167).

The unattainable of every thought process becomes concrete within these webs; thoughts that emerged as confusing and inarticulate attempt to take on a meaningful form. These meaningful thoughts do not remain in their state, however, they have a tendency to keep reproducing, and they create new thoughts. They are, as such, autoproductive aesthetic processes in search of a particular form. "An individual, aesthetically meaningful, thought is despite everything full of internal restlessness" (*VZ,* 21), insists Flusser, as it is driven by an inner dynamic that prevents it from self-sufficiency. This inner dynamic forces thought to give itself up, to overcome itself. But what does this giving up of thinking, of creating another thought, signify other than philosophy? In this sense, the intellect becomes the actual field of doubt. The force behind the web of thoughts is the search for meaning, a meaning that relinquishes itself so that the search can continue and ultimately proves to be absurd. Yet the absurd character of this search—and of philosophy in general—is hardly objectionable.

With an ironic wink, Flusser notes that this is not a metaphorical web; it actually exists and has been woven, or better, thought up, by a philosophical spider. In this game with truth, approximating a hypothetical *Tractatus arachnideus,* the world is only that which happens on the spider's threads. On the basis of this assumption, anything occurring beyond the threads, in the voids in between, does not count as a part of the spider's effective world; the voids present merely possibilities, unrealized potentialities. The events within the voids symbolize the spider's unarticulated, chaotic, and metaphysical pool of philosophy:

> Let's take a moment to stay with this spider. What happens on the threads of the web? There are flies, other spiders, and there are catastrophes that tear the web apart. The spider itself rests in the center of the web. The spider secretes the web and owns it. It moves freely along the web's threads to devour the flies, to mate, to fight other spiders, and to repair damages to the web. Consequently, we can distinguish the following ontological modalities: a fly, another spider, a catastrophe, and the spider itself, with all its complex of problems. (*VZ*, 27–28)

Humans are left with invisible webs that articulate their space, time, emotions, and thought.

The fundamental form of the human web is the sentence. In the case of German, according to Flusser, it follows a subject–predicate structure. Just like the spider's hypothetical web conditions, the spider's thinking, it is not only the sentence that conditions our thinking but reality as such. Language is a creative force; it positions reality inasmuch as it projects meaning onto that which is unstructured. Thinking only happens via language, a conception programmatically enhanced in the titles to the first four parts of *Língua e realidade*: language *is* reality; it forms, creates, and distributes reality. Flusser later expanded and amended this linguistic reductionism, characteristic of his early works, to include more recent aspects of communication theory.

According to Flusser, we cannot escape the subject–predicate structure and the triple ontology derived from it; should we want to, we would have to plummet into the voids of the web. To explain the basic structure of the sentence and this structure's relevance for perceiving reality, Flusser employs a simple sentence: "'The man washes the car.' Man serves as the subject, the car as the object and washes is the predicate. The sentence takes the form of a shot against a screen. We can also compare this situation to the projection of a film" (*VZ*, 27). The subject in this example is the trigger of the sentence, but it fails to suffice in itself. It is a remnant of a previous sentence, searching for its place within a structure of reality that we recognize here as one of language. Taken by itself, this trigger lacks meaning. It is on the lookout for an object with which it can realize itself and become the subject of a new sentence. By itself, and external to any sentence structure, it presents no less and no more than its own search, a self-emanating question. For that reason, we should not write "the man" but rather "the man?" What obstructs the realization of the subject is the object of the sentence, in this case, "the car." The object confronts the subject's search and consequently supplies the subject's search with actual meaning. Taken by itself, the object cannot function as a real object, external to a specific sentence: as something that simply has not been located yet, it awaits an encounter with the subject. Within the sentence, it presents an action sequence for the subject, an imperative. For that reason, we should write "the car!," not "the car." The predicate, here *washes*—its etymology referring back to the Latin *praedicare,* which means "to announce, make known," but also "to predict, prophesy"—implies a movement that points beyond the sentence and toward a project, a projection, a prophesy. For that reason, we should depict it such that its nature as the core of a projection becomes apparent: *washes.*

Subject and object, in this metaphorical reading of the relationship between language and reality, represent not only the two horizons of the sentence but, simultaneously, also those of language and therefore of reality itself. If, based on Flusser's interpretation, the predicate symbolizes in effect the center of the sentence, then it, too, takes position at the center of language and reality, that is, at the center of the web of our thoughts. As a result, we should rewrite the complete sentence as follows: "The man? *washes* the car!" What does Flusser intend to show here? He wants subject and object perceived within their original grammatical context. Subject and object present the horizons of reality of the sentence and therefore guarantee the sentence's continuity. Moreover, he already applies the predicate-based model of language implicitly to the projective and intentional interrelationship of subject and object, that is, of the human being and reality: "Subject, object, and predicate are those forms of being which establish our reality. Let's take a look at the subject, the detonator of the sentence. The subject is not sufficient in itself, it needs a sentence to insert itself into reality." In contrast, "the object is that which hides the project from the subject, it is an obstruction that declares the search finished. It resists the search of the subject and, therefore, assigns the search its meaning. . . . In the sentence, the opposition of subject and object is surpassed by the predicate" (*VZ*, 30–31). And furthermore:

> The intellect proceeds sentence by sentence, and predicate by predicate, eager to exhaust the subject and the predicate and to obtain the entire meaning of the subject and the object, but without success. The intellect proceeds from one partial meaning to another in search of one that is complete but which is never attainable. Thinking is a single enormous predicate of an unpredictable subject directed towards an

unattainable object. . . . Our entire reality consists of this
thinking process, which is the process of language. Our reality is one single unfinished and infinite sentence in search
of unattainable meaning. (*VZ*, 34)

Having Faith in Doubt

We have to acknowledge fundamental doubts to avoid the risk of
having them return as vengeful symptoms because we repressed
them. Nihilism is one of these symptoms. Flusser identifies an
impending nihilism for both our contemporary world and the
greater part of today's thinking. It presents as such the paradoxical
result of, simultaneously, a disproportionate overestimation of
the intellect and an accompanying loss of faith in the intellect's
abilities. The question emerges whether we can actually still
experience reality. Is it still attainable and, with it, our intrinsic
point of reference, or has it become unattainable, just as the
postmodern apostles of the apocalypse predicted?

If we, doubting, obsess about our own doubt, the intellect
intellectualizes itself and blocks the already limited access to
reality. We have two options: either to leave the intellect to its
fate and to take up whichever variation of religious or mystical
anti-intellectualism appears currently in fashion; or to attempt
to examine it instead of giving it up. Flusser chose the second
option and tried to survey the intellect's limits and thereby determine the limits of doubt as well. Significantly, if we cannot
use everything toward a subject or an object in a meaningful
sentence and therefore integrate it into language, not everything
is comprehensible, and if we cannot comprehend everything,
what we can say is limited. The mystery has to be protected.

What we call "reality" is far from obvious, but what we believe, according to Flusser (*DR*, 9), can be inspected and analyzed.
Before Christ's birth, reality was perceived as divine nature; in

the Middle Ages, it took on a transcendent form. Only in the fifteenth century did we problematize the term *reality,* and we turned it into doubt. Nature became a matter of methodical doubt, and faith in a transcendental form was lost. We are thus surrounded by a sentiment of unreality that forces us to search for reality; this search, far from being absurd, in fact uncovers the world's absurdity for us. This conclusion leads many of us to abandon this search and therefore to abandon thinking and doubt as well.

If Descartes doubts to eliminate doubt once and for all from this world, then Flusser doubts to protect doubt as such. Though Flusser acknowledges that thinking at all times contains an irredeemable religious component, he maintains the right to subject this religious dimension to doubt as well. He does not intend to get rid of our religiosity or our right to doubt; rather, quite the opposite: he defends their complicated and precarious coexistence. How does he accomplish that? He recognizes a general willingness to believe without hereby excluding himself. In *Da religiosidade (DR,* 27), he defines the reigning faith of the present as a faith in the concordance of logical thinking with reality and mathematics: the most complete expression of logical thinking lies in the assertions of abstract mathematics as it was codified in algorithmic programming language. For that reason, we believe in the structure of algorithmic language as a last reality. This concordance of reality and logical-mathematical thinking appears, at first, entirely absurd because our everyday life constantly refutes it. Despite such knowledge, however, our faith is prepared, according to Flusser, to recognize this absurd coincidence as an irrefutable fact: we believe, so to say, *quia absurdum.* At the same time, the well-protected and age-old border between religious and scientific worlds is very much in danger.

The Poetical Solution

Despite the critique laid out here, Descartes's methodical doubt is settled comfortably in the innermost quarters of the Occidental thought project. Flusser presents us poetically with our own doubt (*DR*, 33): doubt—and therefore thinking—determines the one who doubts and forces on him or her a particular order, only to have her or him stop doubting and become indubitable. Thinking is an absurd endeavor: he or she is doubted to stop doubting; in the process, the one doubting turns into a dubious being. This process is doubly absurd because the goal of thinking consists of abandoning oneself and because one pretends to reach this goal by dissolving everything with doubt. In that sense, thinking may be compared to a kind of thirst that is to be quenched by drinking up the sea. Yet, of course, were we to drink and empty the sea, we would never finish, and each drop would increase our craving. The more thinking progresses, the more apparent its double absurdity and the fact that we have to pay with the absolute expulsion from paradise. Every time we think and doubt, we are expelled from paradise and from the comfort of our alleged identity. As a result, we are constantly anxious: doubt turns into desperation. To counteract this inner conflict, we need to return to the origins of reality, and for the early, Brazilian, Flusser in *Língua e realidade, Filosofía da linguagem,* and *A história do diabo,* this is language. This return connects to another central thesis of Flusser: language originates with poetry. How so?

The origin of language, for Flusser, consists in the attempt to name things and to appropriate reality via the word. As documented in *On Doubt,* poetry steadily creates language and enriches it, making our comprehension of the world and reality more complex. We do not broaden our understanding of the world through language, by some sort of default, just as language is enriched; quite the contrary: the more we know, the more vast becomes the territory of our ignorance because we only now gain access to that which we do not know. The intellectual project of deciphering the mysterious cannot be subjected to destroy the secret, and the effort to fill the void should not result in eliminating it. The enrichment of language is not followed by an impoverishment of that which cannot be articulated—language expands, but the chaos does not diminish: "Poetry opens up the territory of thinking, but it does not reduce the territory of that which cannot be thought of. Language increases. . . . That which cannot be said remains untouched" (*VZ*, 42–43).

The intellect's field hosts two active and contrary tendencies: a centrifugal, the poetic intuition, producing, that is, supplying the raw material for thought; and a centripetal, the critical conversation, whose task it is to translate proper names into secondary words or to eliminate them from the field of language—proper names either get assimilated, that is, digested, or they are secreted. The intuitive activity produces an expansion of the field, the critical results in its consolidation. Dialogue, the conversation, and poetry, the verse, present the two basic forms of doubt. The intuitive doubt of poetry and the critical doubt of dialogue are responsible for the two basic forms of thinking in the field of the intellect. The intellect has to break through the chaos surrounding and enclosing it for verse to become possible. Here poetical intention collides with that which has yet to be articulated. The specific form of verse refers back to this clash, this creative shock. Verses represent liminal situations in which language tries to overcome itself, to render in words that which cannot be said, to think what cannot be thought, that is, to make nothingness realizable. In this sense, proper names witness the contradictory experience of the intellect's limitations and their simultaneous overcoming.

The Celebration of Thought

Poetry creates language, but our everyday language remains excluded from this process, and not everything may be expressed poetically. Every metaphor surprises reality in the moment of its creation and amazes with a new perspective it has opened up. Everyday use, however, lessens its potential for surprise. The general conversation enables projects of knowledge and invention inasmuch as it flings verse into language; that is, it translates poetry into prose. Yet, in the process, they, too, exhaust themselves and lose layers of their original secret. With conversation's progress, the poetical mystery disappears within a prosaic atmosphere of the habitual. The conversation solidifies thought and gives it stability but remains dependent, ultimately, on poetry. When we detect sites of the poetical and the conversation, we can protect ourselves from arrogant intellectualism as well as desperate anti-intellectualism. What remains most important, to reference one of Flusser's images, is to continue on with weaving the web of Western conversation without assuming that we can catch that which cannot be articulated.

If we believe Flusser, scientific–intellectual activity should not limit itself to explain reality, as in the past, or, as in the present, to aim for a perfect, internal, theoretical consistency; rather it should play with that which cannot be articulated in a celebration of language in philosophy and poetry. The praise of a thought-celebration does not, however, lead to an anesthetized critical mind of the philosopher. Flusser observes in all areas of thinking a daunting combination of dogmatism and pragmatism, delivering political and social systems toward an unethical opportunism. This connection, popular under the name "neoliberalism," accelerates the disintegration of Western conversation; in fact, it paralyzes and numbs potential and active participants. Western conversation seems to dance around a lost sense and to realize itself in ever smaller circles. We talk so much more about so much less. The geometrical growth of information and its accompanying democratization corresponds to a relational decrease of reflection. Especially for that reason, it is necessary to revive the celebration of thought. Offerings were substantially part of it. In Brazil, summer solstice used to be celebrated with an intricately fabricated balloon that was offered to the perfidious wind and to the darkness of the night. The sight of the balloon burning up in the night sky was a reference to the ephemeral and precarious elements of all human endeavors, and at the same time, it was a hymn to the beauty of life.

In the same manner, the human intellect has to offer up its claim to omniscience and control in favor of a smaller intellect, one that knows only as much as it does not know. Such a proposal will probably find few adepts. Nonetheless, only an offering up of modern thought, that is, of methodical doubt in Descartes's succession, is able to protect doubt and the mysteries that provide us with something like beauty. We are required to accept the horizon of doubt and admire it. What has fallen victim to it is the aim of Western conversation, commenced by Descartes and continued by his successors: to render the unthinkable in thought in order to eliminate it from the world. Flusser withstands any intellectualizing, apocalyptic visions and totalitarian materializations by taking part in the celebration of thought. Accordingly, he concludes his treatise *On Doubt*: "Let's continue the great adventure of thought, but let's offer up the proud delusion to control that which is very different *[das ganz Andere]* with our thinking" (*VZ*, 64).

3 | Translation and Multilingual Writing

Theoretical Concept and Creative Principle

Translation is in many respects of major importance in Flusser's life and work: it is at the same time a philosophical concept, a critical tool and creative principle, an art and craft of writing, and a metaphor for a nomadic existence between cultures and continents. Translation serves a specific way of thinking, writing, and living. Flusser wrote most of his texts in two or more of his four writing languages—Portuguese, German, English, and French—continuously translating and retranslating himself. Furthermore, his life, enacted between two continents, can be interpreted as an existence "in translation," in Salman Rushdie's understanding, when he described the rootless lives of the exiled and displaced in a contemporary multicultural global economy. In an interview with Hans Joachim Lenger in Hamburg in 1990, published in *Zwiegespräche,* Flusser sums up his lifelong interest in the subject: "Perhaps everything I do is an attempt to elaborate a theory of translation. But I am not going to live long enough to do that" (ZG, 149).

In the 1960s, Flusser wrote a series of essays about the concept of translation in an attempt to elaborate a comprehensive theory in the field. His extremely ambitious project, at that time, was conceived as a synthesis of Heidegger's existentialism and Wittgenstein's philosophy of language through a theory of translation, reuniting the two main strands of philosophical thinking in the West: the Continental, phenomenological, hermeneutic, and the analytical Anglo-American school. In the late 1960s and early 1970s, he attempted twice to write a longer study on the subject but had to give up, producing drafts of texts only: *Problemas em tradução* [Problems in Translation][1] and *Reflexões sobre a traduzibilidade* [Reflections on Translatability]. He possibly considered Wittgenstein's verdict that any encompassing theory of translation is unattainable as each individual case calls for its own unique theoretical solution, a pragmatic maxim he also applied to his own daily translating activity. Although afterward, the subject of translation practically disappeared from his texts—with very few exceptions—his ideas about translation resurface in many guises in his later communication and media theory and find a practical application in the systematic multilingual writing practice that Flusser expanded and refined in the course of his career, truly one of the most fascinating traits of this multitalented philosopher.

Flusser used the concept of translation not only as a concrete practice to be theoretically analyzed in and of itself but also as a metaphor to be used within and across other fields of research, in his case, philosophy and history as well as communication and media theory. Apart from reconstructing the main lines of Flusser's theory and practice of translation, the main questions to be asked here would therefore have to be as follows: what is the actual relevance of Flusser's ideas on translation for translation studies at large, especially after the cultural turn has reshuffled and redefined the field?[2] In which way could his theoretical and practical heritage inform the ongoing debate? And finally, may Flusser's use of translation help the development of an operational concept of translation within other discursive fields? We are going to deal with some of these aspects in the present chapter and with others in the following one, especially in connection with Flusser's theory of media evolution, which heavily draws on a view of history as a series of translational leaps developed in the 1960s.

Zooming Out

Translation is to be found everywhere in Flusser's work, sometimes in the most surprising guises. It not only represents one of the central moments of his whole philosophical system but it also functions as a sort of hidden principle of writing and rewriting, one of Flusser's most important, if not the most relevant, creative driving force, a *basso continuo* reverberating through his complex, many-layered, labyrinthine work. Flusser's oeuvre could be interpreted as an ever-expanding spiral organized around a few loosely interconnected concepts suspended above an empty, groundless center. Each new writing effort presents an attempt to translate what has already been written into a new context and onto a new level of meaning. The following example shall illustrate this.

Flusser started his writing career from a linguistic theory of reality, moving on to communication and media theory and ending up with a phenomenological theory of gestures. To put it another way, he moved from words in texts to communication processes within specific contexts to embodied thinking expressing itself in gestures. In all three instances, his central point of interest is the communicative intent, the dialogical relevance: the way the words defining and changing our everyday reality can be used to communicate with others; the way messages travel from a sender to a receiver across an intermediate channel and the role media play in this situation; and finally, the way we use gestures to express our being-in-the-world as a way of relating to it and others. The intellectual adventure sketched here is a slow zooming out from an initial position redefining each time the basic tenets. This movement of distancing, stepping back from one's initial position to take in more and more information, thereby constantly widening the scope of vision, is fundamental to Flusser's way of thinking. It connects him to philosophers like Jean Paul Sarte and Martin Heidegger.

Translation and Nomadism

Translation is, in a way, also a constant circling, nomadic movement that never loses sight of its starting point, indeed, always returning back to it to deny and move beyond it again. Flusser's philosophy is a free-floating kind of thinking continuously inventing and reinventing itself by slowly unfolding its subject, constantly setting anchor to break new ground. But at the same time, it always moves back onto itself to follow along its own steps, reconsidering them in the light of newly made experiences. Within this journey, each step is to be understood as a translational jump, the self-reflective turn being a form of retranslation. We will come back to this point later on.

Flusser's thinking is nomadic in that it refuses to be restricted to a clearly defined territory in which it is rooted. Flusser does not want to conquer the space he discovers to build a stable theoretical system. He sets up his tents in a certain area and then moves on. Contrary to other recent concepts of nomadism—for instance, the one developed by Gilles Deleuze—Flusser's thinking insists on the ritualistic and repetitive side of the process. Nomads do not settle in and take over the territory they move through; rather, their movement is never completely free and aimless, insofar as their journeys move along certain tracks and always come back to where they have been. In other words, they do not shoot off tangentially but are basically circular.

This specific form of nomadic thinking is intimately linked to Flusser's practice of translation.

There is no way the original can be completely and exhaustively realized in the translated text. Every translation is a betrayal of the original, and this in a double sense. It never manages to carry over that which is untranslatable, and it always deforms the original by attempting to do so. But if we look at it from another perspective, every translation is at the same time also a form of explication. Translation processes, in fact, tend to increase the semantic relations between the single parts of the translated text, leading to a greater cohesion through repetition, redundancy, and explicitness. Flusser makes use of the idea of radical untranslatability and of the possibilities opened up by the explanatory nature of translation processes. It allows him to develop his work, to move on to farther and farther theoretical horizons, continuously expanding his fields of interest without settling in any one of them. This way, no system can ever establish itself in a specific area of thought. What we are left with is a huge territory crisscrossed with multiple journeys back and forth and a loose shifting, unstable string of interconnected points that bear the trace of previous passages and crossings. To translate a text, then, is above all to criticize it by explicating hidden meaning and adding supplementary points of view. The final text reached through retranslation contains all the new information discovered in the process and sums it up in a new monolingual synthesis. We will return to this aspect again at the end of this chapter.

In Flusser's work, nomadism is also metaphorically linked to a specific notion of translation as a basically endless, open-ended enterprise. The translator is forced to move on continuously, striving at the same time to get back to the origin, only to discover that there is no such possibility. Meaning is homeless and itinerant; it cannot be pinned down in any particular text, not even in the original. But there is more to it. The diasporic nature of any form of meaning is only one side of the game of (re)-translation. Translation unfolds that which is manifold, explicating hidden potentialities of the text. It is, however, also a form of criticism. Flusser translates and retranslates his own texts to check their truth and inner coherence and to criticize his own thinking. Translation, then, is always a twofold process: an evolutive, forward movement, cumulating different points of view, and contradicted and complemented by retranslation, an involutive, backward motion.

Thought and Reflection

This fundamental opposition is also to be found in the use of two other key terms of Flusser's philosophy: *thought* and *reflection*. "Thought," writes Flusser in his essay "Thought and Reflection," is

> the process of grasping which expands into the world of bodies in order to devour them. The methods of this devouring process are science and technology. But there is another direction in which thought can move, namely the opposite direction. In this motion thought turns against itself in order to devour itself, i.e. to understand itself and modify itself. The term "reflection" shows where this kind of thought moves to, namely in the direction opposite to advancing thought. The German term "Nachdenken," (which means "to think behind or after") shows how this kind of thought works, namely as a check on thinking. And finally the Czech term "rozmysleni," (which means "analytical thinking") shows the result of this kind of thought, namely thought dismembered. Reflection is therefore the inverse motion of thought,

wherein thought is being controlled and decomposed into its elements. The method of reflection, which is the devouring of thought by itself, is philosophy. Philosophy is therefore exactly the contrary of science and technology.[3]

We will revisit this basic opposition later as it not only structures Flusser's philosophy of media evolution but is also the underlying principle of his self-translating writing strategy. Before moving on, however, one important detail should be highlighted here.

(Re)-Translation as (Self)-Devoration

In the preceding passage, Flusser introduces the metaphor of devoration that he owes to the *movimento antropófago*—the "cannibalistic movement"—initiated by the Brazilian modernist writer Oswald de Andrade, who published a "Manifesto Antropófago" in the first issue of his *Revista de antropofagia* in May 1928. Andrade used cannibalism as a weapon to replace the image of the passive and submissive Indian with that of the aggressive and rebellious cannibal.[4] His aim was to overcome the country's cultural subservience by reversing the historically imitative stance of Brazilian literature and the one-directional flow of artistic influence. In a way, this represents a postcolonial perspective, long before this school of thought established itself. Flusser complemented this idea by adding another dimension: that of self-devoration, associating it with the self-critical movement of philosophical thinking.

In another passage from his lectures on *Kommunikologie* that he held in the late 1970s at the University of Marseille-Luminy in France, Flusser links these two concepts with the idea of retranslation. He describes the relationship between original and translation in terms of object-language and metalanguage, implying that the source language is always subordinate to the target language. But in the game of translation and retranslation, the relationship between these two languages can always be inverted. One can translate a French text into English and back again into French or simply reverse the procedure. The object-language is fed into a metalanguage, which can in turn be ingested by a second metalanguage." In the case of retranslation," writes Flusser in *Kommunikologie,* "the original relationship of the two codes is reversed: the object-code becomes now a metacode. In other words: after the French code has swallowed part of the . . . English one, it is in turn swallowed by the English code, . . . so to speak with the English in its belly" (*KO,* 343). A complex involuted system of Russian dolls within dolls is created. But there is more to it. In fact, in the course of the translation and retranslation processes, a text ingests and digests another text that is in turn feeding on a text it has previously swallowed. Each new text is an "invitation to a dance," as Flusser puts it in the unpublished Portuguese essay "Retradução enquanto método de trabalho," probably written in the early 1970s in France. "Of course such recurrent coiled retranslation can be formalized. . . . But such a formalization of the problem of retranslation would get rid of the fascination of the game."[5]

One of the decisive theoretical consequences of the possibility of inverting hierarchical settings through translation is the disappearance of a single overreaching, all-embracing metaposition from which to survey and judge all other positions. And Flusser is clearly ahead of his time here. We can find an analogous notion in the work of Wolfgang Iser. Iser calls this principle of hierarchical reversibility "mutuality" and uses it to describe translational processes of cultural formation.[6] The identities of cultures and cultural identities constitute themselves out of continuous processes of mutual assimilation, interpenetration, and superimposition. Iser speaks of a self-regulative form of cross-cultural exchange that has finally liberated itself from any pregiven frames of reference to generate its own control by constantly shifting modes of reference. This cybernetic structure is based on recursive looping, that is, on positive and negative feedback loops—again the feeding metaphor comes up here—which lead to various forms of cultural production.

In Iser's view, furthermore, the relationship between source and target culture is, as with Flusser, a fundamentally reversible two-way flow and therefore never hierarchical. There is, thus, no privileged meta-point-of-view from which to evaluate all other points of view, as any position can be fed into the aforementioned recursive loops of mutuality. As Iser puts it in *The Translatability of Cultures,* "mutuality . . . indicates that there is neither a transcendental stance nor a third dimension that would allow us to conceptualize cross-cultural interrelationships."[7] What we are left with is a series of discrete positions we can nomadically move through, an interconnected net of knots entertaining reversible relationships with each other.

Let me briefly introduce another Flusserian perspective to illustrate this point. The preceding predicament is beautifully summed up in the light-footed dance of the photographer who moves from one point of view to another, slowly circling around her or his object, taking a series of distinct pictures. The sum total of these shots is an attempt to describe the object from as many viewpoints as possible—as in the case of multiple (re)-translation processes.

The Principle of Untranslatability

Flusser's translation theory is inspired by the ideas on language and translation prevalent in the field in the 1960s, but also by Quine's concept of radical translation (asserting the fundamental indeterminacy of translation), by Heidegger's existentialism, by Wilhelm von Humboldt's understanding of language, and by the work of Walter Benjamin, especially the messianic dimension of translation.

The texts of the 1960s deal with translation from two interconnected points of view: an existential and a linguistic. To the first belong the concepts of jump, bridge, abyss, nothingness, death, freedom, and fidelity; to the second belong metalanguage, object-language, and the opposition between grammar as a system of rules and vocabulary as a repository of terms. Some texts stress the existentialistic viewpoint, whereas others focus more on the linguistic perspective. Some others again, such as the one we are going to discuss in the next section of this chapter, "Da tradução (e da morte)," are dedicated to an attempt at synthesis. In all his texts, however, Flusser emphasizes the decisive importance of the concrete practice of translation, the touchstone of all intellectual speculation about the subject.

In "Retradução enquanto método de trabalho," Flusser introduces the idea that the choice of a specific theme is dictated by its (un)-translatability, that is, if it is especially well suited for the game of consecutive translations. "The more difficult it is to translate a certain theme," he writes, "the bigger is the challenge it represents. It causes a dialectical tension between the different languages that inform me, forcing me to look for a synthesis of these contradictions."[8] Translation is thus basically an open-ended process feeding on its own impossibility. We can again draw a parallel here to Iser's view of cultural translation. In *The Translatability of Cultures,* he proposes that "whenever features of culture are translated intra- or cross-culturally, a trace of untranslatability" is inscribed on them. This fundamental incommensurability between cultures does not, however, hamper the communication process itself but "energizes such attempts at comprehension."[9]

In Flusser's thinking, translation is also a model to explain the functioning of cross-disciplinary connections. In an un-published letter written to Hans-Peter Dimke on July 4, 1984, Flusser explains his translational activity as a liberating meta-phoric game: "In order to jump from one medium to another (from one 'universe' to another), I must compare them. . . . This comparison could be called a 'metamedium.' (You would call it 'interdisciplinary.') This metamedium is also a medium, for in-stance, physical chemistry. And then, if you want to be coherent, you would have to jump from this metamedium into another medium. For instance from the metamedium 'photography–painting' into the medium 'music.' In order to do that, you need a metameta-medium. A stepladder completely made out of metaphors. A tremendously enthralling task. Akin to rope dancing or fireworks. I will give you an example: we can trans-late 'sin' from the medium Christianity into Freudian analysis, using the notion of psychological 'complex'; from here we translate it into the Marxist concept of 'alienation' and from there we retranslate it into the Christian term 'belief': so you would have 'sin' = 'belief.' You see the fertility and danger of metaphors."

In view of recent theoretical debates within translation studies, Flusser's notion of a translation-based, discursive in-terdisciplinary endeavor assumes particular importance. In her *Cultural Turns,* published in 2006, Doris Bachmann-Medick has explored the theoretical potentialities of translation to become a sort of metatheory, a *Leitwissenschaft,* capable of unifying the complex field of cultural studies by explaining the functioning of its reversible multiple theoretical exchanges. Accordingly, she asks, could our culturally expanded definition of translation not only help to explain the workings of cross-cultural interactions but also become "a specific model for disciplinary interconnec-tion?"[10] Flusser could definitely assist in such an undertaking.

Synthesis?

A central aspect of Flusser's thinking is his quest for synthesis and unification that assumes many different forms in the course of his career. His first, still unpublished book, written over the course of the 1950s, bears the overambitious title *Das XX. Jahrhundert: Versuch einer subjektiven Synthese* [The Twentieth Century: An Attempt at a Subjective Synthesis]. The index contains six chapters with altogether 150 entries. The single chapters are sometimes only two paragraphs in length. The book, which is only about two hundred pages long, considers practically everything: politics, society, science, art, philosophy, and religion. Flusser reveals himself as an insatiable and omnivorous devourer feeding on interdisciplinary concepts, provocative metaphors, multilingual etymologies, and various other matters. But what exactly does he mean by *synthesis*? In the early work, the concept is pretty close to Gadamer's notion of *Horizontverschmelzung,* implying an effort at homogenization of the heterogeneous. But in later texts, a view stressing difference and discord slowly surfaces. Our guess would be that the two conceptions coexist from the very beginning and that one side of the unequal pair ultimately takes over. Similarly, we have a slow shift from nothingness as a reservoir of unheard-of and unthought-of concepts—the wellspring of creativity from which the intellect extracts new notions—to a conception of nothingness as an empty surface on which we are called to project collective and individual meaning.

Creativity has two sides as well. In an early phase of Flusser's work, it is defined as the creation of something totally different by extracting it from the nothingness that surrounds us: *creatio ex-nihilo.* We can find this view, again in form of the feeding metaphor, in a text from the mid-1960s: *A dúvida* [On Doubt]. Flusser describes in this text the intake of new elements in terms of an amoeba sending out a pseudopodium that engulfs the foreign element with the intention of assimilating it in a slow process of continuous absorption and osmosis. These new elements are not names of classes but proper names, that is, the creation of something utterly unprecedented. The foreign elements that refuse full integration into the body of the amoeba remain undigested. As such they represent a constant challenge to the unity of the system that tries in vain to break them down to assimilate them. Their persistence, however, liberates new creative forces in the process.

Apart from this early view of creativity, insisting on the absolute originality of the unseen and the primary importance of creative subjectivity and individuality, Flusser developed another concept stressing the notions of dialogue and combination. Creativity, then, is never the invention of something absolutely new but always the discovery of unheard-of connections between formerly separated domains. This other form of creativity, let us call it connective and dialogical, *reappears* within Flusser's conceptual pair discourse–dialogue, first *surfacing* in the early 1970s. We will deal more extensively with this in the following chapter and with creativity in chapter 7. It should suffice here to point out that creativity is now seen as the inventive and unusual linking of two preexisting notions. We have thus a shift from a conception based on the singularity of concepts to one focusing on relationship and interaction.

Translation as *ars moriendi*

The word *synthesis* can be found as well in Flusser's early translation theory. In fact, even translation theory itself is a special form of synthesis. In his essay "Da tradução (e da morte)" [On Translation and Death]—published in the *Suplemento literário* of *Estado de São Paulo* on May 26, 1962—Flusser makes use of a metaphorical notion of translation to supplement the missing theoretical link between Russell and Wittgenstein, on one hand,

and Heidegger and Camus, on the other. He proceeds by collating different levels of meaning, that is, by synthesizing the notions of death, abyss, language, and intellect. With Flusser, most of the time content and method mirror and comment on each other. As the title itself graphically suggests, the method used is phenomenological and the point of view subjective: translation allows us to put the experience of death into brackets—it is a metaphorical *epoché* of death.

The intellect is defined as an ensemble of grammatical rules ordering and structuring the chaotic impressions of the *I*. Language thus creates continuity and stability in our perception of the world. Furthermore, each language achieves this structuring experience in its own particular way. This is why languages' essential implications, their kernels, as Flusser calls them, are separated from each other by an unbridgeable abyss. In his early linguistic phase, as one can see, Flusser tends to oversimplify his interpretation by postulating a complete identity between language and reality. This presents the starting point of his argumentation. Flusser continues by linking the different levels of interpretation with a series of metaphorical couplings. The abyss separating the different languages is projected on the chasm existing between life and death and the gap between the two philosophical schools, seen, in this context, as separate languages about reality. The link itself, however, the conceptual bridge, is created by joining the act of translation with death.

Ontologically speaking, death is, as Jaspers put it, the ultimate frontier-experience, or, as Heidegger defined it, the only experience we cannot catch up with *(einholen)* and therefore overcome *(überholen)*. Yet Flusser sees a way to achieve this on a symbolical level, that is, through translation. In fact, when I translate myself, the continuity of the *I* is abruptly interrupted. "But who am I during this process when I translate myself *(me traduzo),* when I cross over *(me traslado)* to another language, when I jump across and I decompose *(decomponho)* myself to recompose *(recompor)* on the bank of the other language?" Flusser interprets this decomposition of the *I* as a symbolic form of death. By studying translation, then, I can learn something about death, even if only metaphorically.

But how can the study of death as translation unite Wittgenstein and Heidegger? Wittgenstein ignores the existential aspect of language; he is not really concerned about translation. His real problem is the tautology of language. Heidegger, on the other hand, ignores the formal aspect of language and concerns himself basically with the impossibility to overcome the notion of nothingness. "The discussion of translation forms a possible bridge between both"—a bridge floating in midair over a bottomless abyss. Translation has both a linguistic and an existential dimension. In the act of translation, our existence overcomes nothingness, and this can consequently be analyzed from a formal point of view. An important aspect here is the complete absence of any mystical overtones. What Flusser is actually looking for is a new sense of reality, a point from which to unravel his work and life. He knew well that this served only as a very tentative way of joining the two philosophical schools and was ultimately doomed to failure. In fact, he dropped any further explicit attempts at a unified theory in the following years, but all his further theoretical work can be viewed from this perspective, an attempt at a final synthesis.

In the autobiographical essay "In Search of Meaning," written in 1969 and published in *Writings,* Flusser summarizes his intellectual career in terms of his translation activity as an existential game between games. The connection to Wittgenstein's theory of *Sprachspiele* is obvious: "Theory of translation is epistemology . . . as Camus knew, the actor, being a translator, is the one who knows. In other words, it must be experienced that everything is art, language, including that utmost game: *ars moriendi.*

It must be translated between games, including the game of death. And this is where, again and surprisingly, rite reappears. Rite as the repertoire of the game of death." Art, music, literature, and philosophy are games, "pieces in my translation game, of a critique that tries to give them meaning. They are open to me. They are my way to play my *ars moriendi*. Of course, this hierarchy may be inverted. To them, I play for them. And in the infinite regression of these invertible hierarchies lies the great question mark, which recedes as translation advances."[11]

Multilingual Writing and Self-Translation

In the course of his life, Flusser developed a multilingual writing style that he extended and improved as he went along. Instead of producing new versions of the text in the same language, he systematically translated it into another language, amending and changing it in the process. In the early stages of his writing career, the 1950s and 1960s, Flusser wrote most of his texts in Portuguese and German, not only single essays but complete books. In the following years, especially after he moved back to Europe in the early 1970s, he added English and French. A few examples will suffice to illustrate this complex writing strategy.

Flusser wrote *A história do diabo* [History of the Devil], published in 1965 in Portuguese, first in German, not being too sure yet of his abilities as a Portuguese writer. The two versions differ quite a lot from each other. The Portuguese variant follows in a loose and very ironical way the chapter structure of Wittgenstein's *Tractatus Logico-Philosophicus*. Flusser's collection of essays dedicated to everyday objects, *A coisas que me cercam* [Things That Surround Me], was written around 1970. There are three different but not identical versions in German, English, and Portuguese. The philosophical fable *Vampyrotheutis infernalis,* first published in German in 1987, exists in two German and two Portuguese versions alongside a series of shorter English texts.

The most striking example of this writing practice, however, is the first chapter of *Posthistory*, a book Flusser wrote in the early 1980s. "The Ground beneath Our Feet" exists in altogether twelve different versions—two English, five Portuguese, four German, and one French—that can be ordered into two consistent textual lines. The first sequence consists of four texts in four different languages; the second, on the other hand, of one English, four Portuguese, and three German texts. The text itself focuses on Auschwitz and its larger cultural consequences. There is a major thematic shift to be detected between the two sequences. Flusser has moved a few paragraphs around, focusing more decidedly on the notion of apparatus and its deadly consequences. The unusually high amount of different versions could be explained by the importance of the topic, as Auschwitz not only stands for one of the possible starting points of a posthistorical situation, according to Flusser, but symbolically also represents the very place where Flusser's whole family disappeared and his personal exile was initiated, a deadly abyss swallowing all meaning, the void origin of *Bodenlosigkeit* (groundlessness or rootlessness)— essentially, the beginning and foundation of his philosophy.

The practice of self-translation, as already pointed out before, is to be understood above all in the sense of a critical reassessment in an attempt to expand and deepen the multiple meanings of the text, each new version adding new aspects. In the end, the last text, having assimilated all the changes through repeated acts of translation, is retranslated into the language of the first version, and the two versions are finally read alongside each other. This way, the unfolding, forward movement is always checked by a contrary backward motion, thought and reflection. Self-translation is a self-critical ballet, a snake biting its own tail, a spiral closing in on itself. If the solution reached is more or less satisfactory, the text will be published; otherwise, the dance will begin again. The publication of a text, however, is a profoundly ambiguous act in a way, embodying only a temporary compromise as no text is final; in fact, it is no more than a provisional stage reached in the course of a fundamentally endless, open-ended, nomadic thinking process.

To describe the final outcome of his writing activity, the copresence of all previous texts within the last, Flusser used the image of a palimpsest, suggesting that in the empty spaces between the written lines and the intervals between the single words and letters, as well as in this text's overall textual arrangement, the other texts still live on in some sort of way. As he puts it in the unpublished English version of *The Gesture of Writing,* this palimpsest is "not readily decipherable, but still in a sense effective."[12] In a parallel French version of the same text, he uses the word *vestiges,* meaning "remnants," "leftovers," and pointing thus to an archaeological dimension of multilingual writing. The written page is a many-layered space of lines within lines within lines that the reader is asked to dig up in an endless movement of deciphering. She will have to look for the traces left by the process of translation and retranslation, the invisible plurilingual content hiding beneath the monolingual text of the last version, the different layers of the final multilingual palimpsest mirroring the manifold complexity of the original thought.

This method recalls a specific practice of the Jewish Kabbalah which consists in a vertical interpretation exploring endlessly receding spaces of boxes within boxes or, to use an architectural metaphor, rooms within rooms. Flusser is using here an archaeological imagery, describing the final text in terms of one stratum overlying the other, implying that beneath each single stratum, another underlying layer can be glimpsed, the very last opening up onto the nothingness from which the original thought has emerged. The best way to experience fully the complexity and diversity of Flusser's thinking would therefore probably be a parallel multiple reading of the same text in its different versions.

Translation and Identity

We would like to end this chapter on the notion of translation in Flusser's work by focusing very briefly on its significance for the constitution of cultural identity, another theme that has been discussed intensely within translation studies in the last decades. Living between continents and cultures, Flusser has always led an existence "in translation." As early as 1966, he published the essay "Barroco Mineiro visto de Praga" in the *Jornal de Commercio*.[13] The structure of this text is a complex movement of translation and retranslation between Prague and the Baroque buildings of Ouro Preto, remindful of Iser's concept of mutuality. Flusser weaves back and forth between the two sites, discussing his own cultural identity as an endless swinging of the cultural pendulum, a swinging that will not stop. Influenced by the historical Baroque of seventeenth-century Prague, he is at first appalled by the apparent artificiality of its Brazilian variant dating from the late nineteenth century. But in the course of his analysis, the initial cultural hierarchy between Europe and South America, motherland and colony, original and copy, source and target language, object-language and meta-language, suddenly swivels, and the artificial Brazilian version is suddenly used to expose the artificiality of the original. Such clever cross-cultural reading is of great significance for present-day translation theory and deserves much more attention than it has received within the field.

Flusser did not develop his linguistically and existentially inspired translation model any further in the 1970s and 1980s. He simply extended its application to the new fields of com-munication and media theory, converting it thus into a general metaphor for transformative processes. The metaphor of translation underwent what we might call an unchecked inflationary career. In the course of the last decades, a growing number of translation theorists have come to discard the purely linguistic view of the process of translation, expanding it into an ethical and political act of intercultural communication. Conversely, ethnologists, literary critics, and historians have come to use the notion of translation in new—not only metaphorical—ways, viewing cultural and social negotiations as acts of translation. Both tendencies have led to an expansion and redefinition of the term *translation* in its relation to cultural and interdisciplinary contexts. This redefinition, however, also has its problematic side. In fact, as Flusser's work shows, the constant expansion of the meaning of the notion of translation threatens to drain it of its content and, therefore, of its operability.

To counteract this dangerous development, Bachmann-Medick suggests a three-step plan: after having amplified the scope of research, and following a phase of metaphorization, a "methodical profiling" is needed.[14] This is exactly the point where Flusser's own work and the theoretical situation of present-day culturally inspired translation theory converge and meet. It is for this reason that, despite Flusser's obvious limitations, the scope and originality of his ideas is still wide and differentiated enough to be of inspiration for contemporary translation studies. At a time when translation studies were still dominated by the subordination of the translated text to the original, and when the role of the translator was still defined in terms of invisibility, as Lawrence Venuti has shown in *The Translator's Invisibility*,[15] Flusser was already practicing a form of translation and formulating a general theoretical, translational framework that was based on transformation, not equivalence: an approach and a practice that has only nowadays become common.

4 | Cultural Studies and Phenomenology

Vilém Flusser's work has been squeezed into a number of disciplines and areas, most of which he would have ogled with some suspicion, rejected outright, or accepted only reluctantly as a home for his ideas and work. Most likely, he would have accepted the label "philosophy" for his writings, albeit with reservations: "Mine was a life without religion and in search of religion, and is this not, after all, a definition of philosophy? . . . I am a failure, because I live philosophy. Which is to say that philosophy is my life."[1] Yet numerous philosophers might tend to object to this label and designate his essayistic musings as anything but serious philosophy. In most of the Western world—at least the cultures and traditions that have taken note of him—and to some degree in Brazil, he has risen to status in media theory. This is ironic, especially because he stubbornly hammered away on old typewriters until he died. Certainly his arguments related to computers, to different media, to how we see and are seen—particularly photography and film—and to how images affect our thinking are easily subsumed under the category "media theory"; hence he can be comfortably placed within the disciplinary homes of communication studies or media studies. However, his interest, his focus, is not the media and the apparatuses but human be-ings. Human beings and their ability to create and to think, to change themselves and the world around them, are at the center of his prolific oeuvre. What his work is not limited to is one area of inquiry or a single discipline within which it would find a convenient or comfortable home.

Indeed, his intellectual development and output complement his biography: an exile and migrant in life, he was a migrant in thought as well. Because, to some extent, he worked within the Jewish–scholarly tradition of synthetic and critical commentary, and because he was marked by his rootless biography, his writ-ing resulted in a certain synthetic rootlessness. He rarely cited his sources, and he rarely acknowledged those who influenced his thinking. What he chose to do, rather, was dwell in the mul-tiple cultures, languages, and ideas that, in essence, held him together as a young man and into old age. Having "survived, groggily, the bestial and stupid earthquake of Nazism, which devoured my world," he, with time, began to realize his pos-sibilities in Brazil:

> My German culture persisted, but gained a new coloring: he who dwelled within the nucleus of myself was my enemy. My Czech culture persisted, too, but as if condemned to smothering by amputation of the umbilical cord that had linked me to it. My Jewish tradition . . . acquired a much greater importance than before, and at the same time was put to a severe test that it hardly stood. . . . And the appeals of Zionism . . . did not reach me sufficiently to commit me. They were all held in check by the appeals of my Brazilian surroundings.[2]

Flusser, the exile and migrant, became a migrant in thinking and writing, breaking down the limitations of disciplinary work and methodologies simply by ignoring them altogether. His ideas, his languages, his work had no real intellectual home.

Flusser's approach to inquiry, to thinking, and to research became an expression of, and parallel to, the uncertainties he had to confront in his life. As apparent from chapter 2 of this volume, doubt and uncertainty, however, contain or give rise to specific liberties as well. Flusser had questions, he observed, he read, and he wrote precisely because he learned that nothing was certain and that doubt also facilitated intellectual agility, permitting travel between cultures, languages, and disciplines. In that sense, science and the objectivity required for its pursuit and presentation symbolized to Flusser precisely the kind of establishment he sought to question. Limitations, frames, closed spaces (or minds), and impenetrabilities served no intellectual purpose whatsoever, and he preferred to live—oftentimes uneasily—in the "between-spaces" or beyond the "between" rather than get or remain trapped in one geographical or epistemological location. In a 1990 interview, he was adamant about the absurdity of borders:

> There is no border line. There are no two phenomena in the world that could be divided by a boundary. It would always be a bad and artificial separation. Phenomena cannot be separated in this way. They also cannot be organized according to straight lines. Phenomena overlap, they happen in layers. I have to point out that in French "border" is used as a military term: the front. Let's hope that the idea to set boundaries everywhere will wear away: this is a man, this is a woman, this is Germany, and this is France. There are no whites, no blacks, no pure cultures, and no pure disciplines. Every systematic thinking is wrong, every system is a violation. Reality is tangled and therefore interesting. Every Cartesian thinking that creates order is fascist. (ZG, 97)

And in that, his work approaches an area of inquiry that is none because it goes beyond borders, it prescribes no precise disciplinary limits, and perhaps, infuriatingly, it lacks a center, too: cultural studies.

Elements of Cultural Studies in Flusser's Work

Despite its centrifugal characteristics, the focus of cultural studies, generally speaking, has remained the study and analysis of culture, more precisely, conjunctures. These can be described as circumstances and constellations that are intricately intertwined with the critical questions posed, the things examined, and the positions taken, no matter whether we speak of "two cultures" (C. P. Snow), many, or one. Whereas Nelson, Treichler, and Grossberg worked within a broad scope of cultural studies, defining the subject as "committed to the study of the entire range of a society's arts, beliefs, institutions, and communicative practices,"[3] Chris Barker defines the more precise moment of conjunctural as "a form of analysis which is historically and contextually specific. An exploration of the assemblage, coming together or articulation of particular forces, determination or logics at specific times and places."[4] His definition is a fancier way of expressing of what Raymond Williams reminds us: "You cannot understand an intellectual or artistic project without also understanding its formation." This "exploration of the assemblage" and of the formation of projects, beginning with the dismantling of the surface, was of great concern to Vilém Flusser throughout his life and work. For our purposes, we begin at the end of it to classify him more accurately as a practitioner of cultural studies. The space for this exploration, for the "assemblage" of Flusser as a cultural studies philosopher, is perhaps, of course, limited. However, this discussion may inspire additional archeologies, contextualizations, and inquiries that can serve to challenge the fossilized reception of Flusser as primarily a media and communications theorist—a reception that is beginning to break open.

In his Bochum lectures on communicology, Flusser put forth the image of a child with a doll. The child rips open the doll's belly to see what it may find inside. This constitutes an act of criticism, according to Flusser, and he himself would like to "rip open the belly of culture to see which communicological circuits are hidden therein." For his purposes, he defined *culture* as follows: "Culture is the kind of device whereby received information can be saved in order to be accessed." This device culture needs to be criticized, and "an important criterion of cultural criticism is a balance between discourse and dialog."[5] It quickly becomes evident that Flusser built his construct of culture on familiar territory with regard to terminology, which includes memory, society, translation, and the end of objectivity. If we trace this analysis of culture back to his earliest texts, we realize how much of a role the concept has played for him already and that we are confronted with overlaps, translations, and transgressions concerning cultural studies inquiries and, specifically, conjunctural knowledge. In fact, in so doing, we shall identify three fundamental elements in Flusser's intellectual work that we can also ascribe to cultural studies practices:

1. First is a theoretical approach that loathes borders or limitations of any kind, apparent in the types of questions posed and in the texts written: Flusser refuses to be "disciplined" in his thought and in his compositions. This applies to both methodological and linguistic aspects, which, as we explain in chapter 3, become part of Flusser's analysis of culture.

2. Second is the observation of phenomena, primarily inspired by Husserl and carried into his theory of photography, for example, by considering the "swarm of positions"

surrounding the phenomena, thereby overcoming the limits of objectivity and of limited vantage points, that is, the limits of ideological valuation.

3. Third is a decided interest in what Chris Barker has called an "inquiry that explores the production and inculcation of maps of meaning": Flusser plunges beneath the surface, he rips open cultural geographies to shed light on the foundations of culture and that which we describe as cultural knowledge or value systems, in his case, the structures of communication and languages, and in conjunction with these structures, the human being in his cultural context.

The Possibilities of the Transfinite

These three elements need to be mapped out in greater detail. Concerning the absence of borders in Flusser's work (element 1), it is apparent from Flusser's multilingualism that he lived, thought, worked, and wrote in terms that are transfinite. He did not stay within some form of *bilanguaging* or "border thinking," as theorized by Walter Mignolo: "Languaging is not a replacement of Humboldt's *energeia* but rather 'a way of life.' . . . Now, since languaging is interacting *in* language and language is what allows for describing and conceiving languaging, bilanguaging then would be precisely that way of life between languages: a dialogical, ethic, aesthetic, and political process of social transformation rather than energeia emanating from an isolated speaker."[6] Flusser moved beyond border thinking because, for Flusser, living, thinking, working, and writing in several languages, in several disciplines, and in several countries did not present some sort of fracturing of existing hegemonies with the promise of "new critical horizons." It presented postfascism, the only possibility for an intellectual life after Auschwitz.

The reasons are manifold. When Flusser asked himself,

"wherefrom do I think?" he entered multicultural and multilingual territory that—to him—had no borders, nor did it present a home. In language and ideology, he was familiar with the colonial histories of the Occident, and he was just as familiar with the subaltern niches of marginalized cultures and cosmologies: as a Jew, as a central European, and as an immigrant to Brazil, a culture whose subalternity he sensed, a country that was stuck in border thinking. He got only so far in his efforts to communicate his travels in this territory because the required translation work was laborious:

> I was born in Prague, and my ancestors appear to have lived in the Golden City for more than a thousand years. . . . For decades now I have taken part in the attempt to synthesize a Brazilian culture out of a mixture of Western and Eastern European, African, East Asian, and Indian cultural elements. I now live in a village in Provence, and I have become assimilated into the weft and warp of this timeless place. I was brought up in the German culture, and I have reconnected with it over the past several years. In short, I am now without heimat because too many heimats reside within me. This manifests itself daily in my work. I feel at home in at least four languages, and I feel challenged and even forced to translate and then back-translate everything that I write. (FM, 1–2)

Essentially, translation as such becomes infinite, as Rainer Guldin has pointed out: at the center of Flusser's theory of translation is the "moment of radical continuity of all translation work, no matter whether they relate to the process of identity formation or the act of multilingual writing."[7] In her study on the correlation between translation and transnation, Emily Apter expands this notion and turns translation theory into a political issue under the auspices of cultural studies: "Envisaged as the source of an ambitious mandate for literary and social analysis, translation becomes the name for the ways in which the humanities negotiate past and future technologies of communication, while shifting the parameters by which language itself is culturally and politically transformed."[8] Flusser would place very prominently within this reading of translation, especially regarding his identity and practice as a migrant in languages and cultures as well as in disciplines. His questioning of positions taken and of knowledges distributed concerns languages, cultures, cosmologies, and epistemologies in numerous areas. It mattered greatly to him how we build knowledge and memory, how we administrate both, and that we find out whether and how they are still significant to us and others.

Flusser best portrayed his factual and metaphorical existence as a migrant in languages, cultures, hegemonies, and epistemologies in his essay "The Challenge of the Migrant," quoted earlier, a text we suggest be read through the lens of cultural studies. The magnitude he assigned to homelessness stands in direct correlation to the impossibility of borderlines between languages, between nations and cultures, and between memories and knowledges. And the "foreigner," categorized as such, stands in direct opposition to the repulsiveness of those who are settled, to the monolingual, to those "experts" drawing borderlines between territories of knowledge and memory. More significantly, his questioning of borders implies a questioning of the meaning of "freedom" that arises from severing one's ties to a "heimat":

> The feeling for heimat, so celebrated in prose and poetry, this mysterious rootedness in infantile, fetal, and transpersonal regions of the psyche, cannot withstand the sober analysis that he who is without heimat is duty bound and able to

undertake. . . . But after the transformation of expulsion into the dizziness of freedom and the inversion of the question "Free from what?" into "Free for what?" . . . , the mysterious rootedness comes to be seen as obscurantist enmeshment that must be cut through like a Gordian knot. . . . He then realizes not only that each heimat blinds in its own particular way those who are enmeshed in it, and that all heimats are equal in this sense, but also that clear judgment, decision making, and action become possible only after one sees oneself clear of this enmeshment. (FM, 4)

The migrant becomes her own home from which she can build networks with others, out of the home's perforations and with the dialogue she makes possible. Flusser called this a "creative house" that serves as "a knot of the interpersonal network."[9]

As such, the migrant also joins the nomads, another concept Flusser developed in various essays. It is a concept that is closely related to both his criticism of Western historiography and his ripping open of cultural geographies in that the nomad embodies the ultimate criticism toward a territorialized point of view: "Only now that we cannot be labeled, cannot be classified and rubricated, only now that we are no longer settled, can we experience what is essential about ourselves. This means that we can experience ourselves as embedded in a concrete relationship, as the Other of an Other" (FM, 48–49). In fact, in one of his interviews, he pointed out that "nomadism is anarchy" (ZG, 107). This kind of experience, of course, refers back to the network Flusser viewed as emerging from the freedom to choose one's ties as a migrant—or the freedom to cut them again as a nomad. This network, constituted not by bonds into which one is born but by bonds that one constructs in proximity with others and their ideas, has transfinite possibilities.

Multiplicity of Perspectives

Concerning the swarm of positions surrounding a phenomenon in postobjective and postteleological scientific approaches (at least in the humanities and social sciences) further adds to Flusser as a practitioner of cultural studies (element 2). The list of names with whom we could compare Flusser's ideas on this issue would be too long to cite here, but we can determine a list of focal points or terms that play an important role for both Flusser and other cultural studies representatives, for example, *language, identity, experience, history, memory, writing. Code* is a more concrete example and prominent for Flusser, who was particularly interested in the transition from the alphanumerical to the digital code. To Flusser, this transition implicated a new understanding of critique: critique becomes a synthesized practice, based on knowledge that is interdisciplinary and part of a network of knowledges. He stipulated in *Does Writing Have a Future?* "We will have to learn to rethink our entire history. Backwards and forwards" (*WF*, 146). The future reader is not limited to knowledge that has been accumulated in linear time, but he can broaden the appropriation of understanding by learning more flexibly, by creating nets and making connections, by analyzing conjunctures that defy a strictly linear examination.

Flusser isolated a particularly thorny conjuncture when examining the critique of images:

> If we consider how the criticism of images has been elaborated during the course of our history, then critical thinking cannot be applied to photography or other technical images, because these images are based on science and technology—produced by apparatuses—and are therefore themselves based on critical thinking. . . . Technical images force critical thinking to turn against itself. . . . In terms of

photography and other technical images, critical thinking is in crisis. It is being pressured to elaborate new criteria, to critique the myths projected into the world by photographs and the particular magic that results from photography. For these myths and this magic have themselves been produced by critical thinking. . . . In short, my thesis is: critical thinking is presently experiencing its own crisis because it does not possess the appropriate criteria allowing it to critique its own products.[10]

Our conundrum, according to Flusser, is that the circle of knowledge and inquiry is closing in on itself, and we have turned critique into magic, a seemingly contradictory situation. One of the concepts that helped Flusser analyze this situation is that of the code. An important element in Flusser's philosophy, it has also long been a cultural studies phenomenon that Chris Barker describes as "a system of representation by which signs and their meanings are arranged by cultural convention to temporarily stabilize significances in particular ways."[11] In *Gesten,* for example, especially the chapter on the "Gesture of Searching," Flusser's idea of a code becomes more concretely phenomenological, that is, material, and we see here, too, commonalities with, and translations of, a cultural studies–oriented material history or material studies. Flusser proposed that "all our gestures (our acts and our thoughts) are structured by scientific inquiry and that our gestures change, if they do change, because the gesture of searching is on the brink of change" (*GE,* 199). With this thesis, he asks us that we acknowledge ourselves as gestures, that we recognize ourselves in a specific context—the relational moment—and that we abandon the differentiation between subject and object. Presumably, many cultural studies practitioners would agree with Flusser's thesis; yet he took it further by adding the term *proximity* and connecting interest or curiosity and reality. The "interest [of the scientist / the searcher], the 'proximity' becomes the measure for reality" whereby one draws "a map for orientation" (*GE*, 211).

Bill Brown, editor of *Things,* describes this orientation as follows: "The real, of course, is no more phenomenal in physics than it is in psychoanalysis. . . . Somewhere beyond or beneath the phenomena we see and touch there lurks some other life and law of things, the swarm of electrons. Nonetheless, even objects squarely within the field of phenomenality are often less clear . . . the closer you look."[12] The act of mapping appears more and more to be a chance for getting lost in the process of seeing or knowing, which, of course, happens always to be a by-product of (re)-searching. By referring to Arjun Appadurai's *The Social Life of Things,* Brown emphasizes, just like Flusser, the questioning of one's position subsequent to the questioning of things: what is needed are "questions that ask not whether things are but what work they perform—questions, in fact, not about things themselves but about the subject–object relation in particular temporal and spatial contexts . . . to grant [objects] their potency—to show how they organize our private and public affection."[13] The entanglement of the subject with the object correlates with the relational moment of conjuncture, just as with Flusser's idea of code or gesture. The (re)-seacher is being redirected toward the more or less clear map for his or her orientation, but he or she is, simultaneously, also responsible for (re)-creating it.

Elsewhere, and in connection with Edmund Husserl, Flusser elaborated quite clearly how the notion of subject–object relations comes to bear on human relations in society. Here, too, Flusser's ideas on media theory were born out of his curiosity to analyze human beings and their behavior, not the other way around: "Under a phenomenological perception, society will be seen as a network composed of *intersubjective* intentional relationships. There is nothing concrete about the individuals that comprise society: if they are unknotted, they will disappear. 'I' am the sum of my concrete relationships (a father, a writer, somebody's friend, a taxpayer); if all these relationships are removed, nothing will remain. . . . On the other hand, there is nothing concrete about society: if the knots that compose it are unknotted it will simply disappear."[14] The singular vantage points that have disappeared in that society are nothing but a network of relations that cannot be approached, analyzed, and described only from above or below; it requires a multiplicity of perspectives to understand how it constructs and reconstructs itself, how its inner workings are changed or repeated. Flusser took this opportunity to introduce his notion of the telematic society, which originated from Husserl's ideas:

> Telematics may be defined as a technique which builds channels (cables and so forth) that carry intersubjective intentionalities from one individual to another. A telematized society will be exactly that network of pure relationships which Husserl defines as the concrete structure of the social phenomenon. . . . What goes on in such a society is a constant dialogue between all men. . . . We can see, then, in what sense it may be said that Husserl has done away with humanism. Instead of the individual man being the supreme value, it is now the dialogue between men that becomes the supreme value, or what Martin Buber . . . calls the "dialogical life" (das dialogische Leben).[15]

Any inquiry, any search for meaning, any new mapping to orient oneself, therefore becomes a kind of swarming around these knots that channel ongoing dialogues between members of a society. One position, one vantage point has become obsolete, and the multiplicity of perspectives and meaning constitutes part of (telematic) society. It is here that the telematic society, in its Husserlian inflection, reflects Flusser's entire work as an almost-system and where David Woodruff Smith's description of Husserl's oeuvre approximates Flusser's:

> Husserl's texts are like holographic plates, or rather chunks of the whole plate that contains Husserl's systematic philosophical image of consciousness and the world. Husserl's whole philosophical system is visible in each of his texts, although each text focuses on specific themes of phenomenology, ontology, logic, and so on. So the system is a hologram. Reading Husserl on one theme reignites the image of his whole system, inviting the reader to look more closely into other parts of the system.[16]

In Flusser's almost-system, the plates and the hologram would also be moving and in flux.

Geographies of Culture

Concerning getting into the "assemblages" that manufacture "maps of meaning" and dissecting the "formation" of a project (element 3), Flusser pursued a number of practices. His practice of ripping open cultural geographies frequently occurred in conjunction with the interplay between dialogue and discourse, for example, terms Flusser used constantly and that are explained further in our chapter on media theory (chapter 5). We can determine overlaps with several practitioners of cultural studies here, and I shall refer only to one of them, Homi Bhabha, before laying out additional texts of Flusser's on the matter.

Bhabha is of particular interest in combination with Flusser, especially because Flusser also added—in his own way—to the diversity of postcolonial voices. Bhabha and Flusser already agree on interdisciplinarity, borders, and the metaphoricity of translation, as is apparent from this excerpt of "Dissemination":

Interdisciplinarity is the acknowledgment of the emergent sign of cultural difference produced in the ambivalent movement between the pedagogical and performative address. . . . In the restless drive for cultural translation, hybrid sites of meaning open up a cleavage in the language of culture which suggests that the similitude of the *symbol* as it plays across cultural sites must not obscure the fact that repetition of the *sign* is, in each specific social practice, both different and differential. This disjunctive play of symbol and sign make interdisciplinarity an instance of the borderline moment of translation that Walter Benjamin describes as the "foreignness of languages."[17]

Bhabha's comparison of the performative and the pedagogical, in particular, could produce a fruitful discussion when examining Flusser's understanding of dialogue and discourse. Bhabha, for example, observes a splitting between the "continuist, accumulative temporality of the pedagogical, and the repetitious, recursive strategy of the performative";[18] that is, within the discourse of the nation (lodged in the past, ideologically inclined and essentialist), the people become an object; in the present, through dialogue and interpersonal performance, the diverse population becomes subjective and autonomous, the kind of accumulation of knots that channel dialogue of human beings rather than making the individual the supreme entity.

Flusser, in turn, built an ambivalence of liminality around these two terms (toward a networking with the other, based on his notion of proximity), the various stages of which we have to pass through. Here we could also include Mignolo's notion of border thinking that provides us with another reading of Flusser not as a postcolonial thinker but as a philosopher or practitioner of cultural studies in a postcolonial culture such as Brazil. For Brazil, its cultural history and its simultaneity of cultures, ethnicities, and identities, proved fascinating to Flusser, and despite his doubts and eventual departure, he wrote about this interplay in numerous essays and in his 1994 book *Brasilien oder die Suche nach dem neuen Menschen* [Brazil or the Search for a New Human]. In his "philosophical autobiography," *Bodenlos*, he tried to reconstruct his decision to move beyond his suicidal phase in the 1940s and to engage with Brazilian culture by attempting to approach culture via his "beyond-border thinking":

> Once one has transcended one's own culture (that is, one has lost one's footing) a different kind of cultural experience becomes possible. One hovers above a whole set of cultures, and at the same time one is consciously experiencing this drifting. One can perceive how the different cultures interconnect with each other, how they form groups and hierarchies, how they distance themselves from each other, how chasms open up between them and how they fight against each other. And at the same time one experiences the impossibility to assess cultures, that is, to choose between them. One perceives oneself adrift, and since one starts viewing oneself as an "I" created by one of the cultures that one has transcended, the drifting itself is experienced as a progressive transcending of one's self, as a progressive self-estrangement. (This is an aspect of playing with suicide that has been referred to earlier.) (*BO*, 77)

Getting below the surface of Brazil's historical and cultural construction, however, proved no easy feat for Flusser, and examining the mapping of what frequently presented itself as impenetrable remained an intriguing challenge. He commenced by letting Brazil's interior, its gargantuan nature, seduce him, only to find that many a Brazilian writer and intellectual, among them João Gimarães Rosa, had already done so. Eventually, he realized that he will get to the layers beneath the surface of Brazilian cultures only via the knots that he was building in the 1950s and 1960s and that he could only examine the assemblage and the formation of projects by making himself part of the system of channels and cables that constituted Brazilian society.

He explained this process in his essay on homelessness: "Everyone was a pioneer in this no-man's land [Brazil]. In my own case, a Brazilian philosophy still had to be elaborated in concert with other comrades who shared my fate. And so we began to spin out dialogical threads between ourselves, ones that we did not inherit at birth in our lost heimats, but ones that we freely produced" (*FM*, 9). By engaging in this process—and it is closely related, of course, to his thoughts on Husserl and society—Flusser was, with time, able to develop a theory of culture and society that incorporated his concepts of code and memory, most notably in an essay on "The Loss of Faith" and in one of his last texts, *Vom Subjekt zum Projekt* [From Subject to Project]. Here Flusser moved beyond the immediate autobiographical influences on his thought and began to concentrate his focus on the human as project. In "The Loss of Faith," he emphasized that "neither does 'spirit' constitute a product of culture, nor does 'culture' constitute a spiritual product; rather, both, culture and spirit, are aspects of a 'field' of information processes."[19] To him, then, these information processes consisted of codes, or they could be codified, leading to the construction of cultural memory that needed to be scrutinized: "Codified information that is not in the program of a given society will not be accepted by this society as information."[20] The relevancy of "ripping open cultural geographies" is directly related to the decoding of information and led Flusser to question the formation of codes and the methods of storing codes and establishing hierarchies of codes. Although we may now have returned to the late Flusser, a media theorist in appearance, the philosopher's formation and assemblage correlate to a cultural studies project and a phenomenology all his own.

In an infrequently read essay, published in 1991, Flusser fully established his status as a practitioner of cultural studies and a phenomenologist. In "Aesthetic Education," Flusser has us consider the "Paleolithic human" who was raised to become an *uomo universale* so that no one had to bother anymore with the "classical division between the so-called three 'ideals,' the true, the good, and the beautiful."[21] However, much more information accumulated, the knowledge of human beings became specialized by default, and no one was able to be "competent for the entire culture." Flusser did not identify specialization as the problem, a specialization necessary for the benefit of control and for the benefit of administering masses of information on culture; rather he had problems with the word *competent*. According to Flusser, generalists should be educated with the help of artificial memories because the goals of education are not "contemplative philosophers but active producers of new information, that is, participants active in accumulating more culture." By referring to aesthetics as the teaching of experience *(Erleben),* Flusser vehemently advocated for a trans- and interdisciplinary work and called it a "dialogic, intersubjective creation." It is a form of cultural studies and phenomenology he pursued passionately until the end.

5 | Communication and Media Theory

Communication and Death

In the first chapter of *Kommunikologie,* written in the early 1970s and bearing the title "What Is Communication?," Flusser sketches the most salient aspects of his communication theory. He considers human communication from an existential point of view, the question being, why do we communicate at all? We communicate not so much to exchange information between a sender and a receiver linked by a channel as to create with others a reason for living. Communication is an artificial, intentional, dialogic, collective act of freedom, aiming at creating codes that help us forget our inevitable death and the fundamental senselessness of our absurd existence. In the classic communication model of sender and receiver, the attention is focused on how to carry the message safely across with as little loss and modification as possible. How can I reduce misunderstandings—due to difficulties of interpretation—and interferences in the channel, for instance, noise? Flusser, in contrast, focuses on the question, how do we manage to create, store, and distribute information to make our condition as human beings acceptable?

We create a web of information to understand and interpret

the world around us and ourselves in connection with others, only to lose sight in a second moment of realizing its artificial nature. Culture thus becomes a nature of second degree. Flusser describes this process of gradual forgetting on pages 3 and 4 of the English version of the text, included in Andreas Ströhl's 2002 anthology *Writings*: "People are not always fully conscious of the artificial character of human communication. . . . After learning a code, we have a tendency to forget its artificiality. If one has learned the code of gestures, then one no longer recognizes that head nodding signifies yes only to those who make use of this code. . . . In the last analysis, the purpose of the codified world is to make us forget that it is an artificial texture that imbues our essentially meaningless, insignificant nature with significance according to our needs. The purpose of human communication is to make us forget the meaningless context in which we are completely alone and incommunicado, that is, the world in which we are condemned to solitary confinement and death: the world of 'nature.'" This problem is particularly manifest with monolingual people who tend to equate their language with the world at large. Bilingual or multilingual people, on the other hand, know from personal experience that reality is not one but rather always appears in different heterogeneous versions. As Flusser ironically and pointedly put it, it rains differently in English and Portuguese. Unity is thus shattered once and for all, and a sense of the fundamental artificiality of all reality comes about. In this context, translation becomes a (self)-critical exercise reminding us of the unbridgeable abysses lying between the different realities around us.

With his communication theory, Flusser wants to draw attention to the ultimate artificiality of all codes, communicative structures and media, and culture at large and to their constructivist side. Humans create culture to liberate themselves from the fear of death but, nonetheless, create only a new form of dependency. This cultural dialectic which transforms any act of rebellion and freedom into an act of submission and defeat holds true not only for codes but for all other human creations as well. As Flusser puts it further down in "What Is Communication?," "the web that is supposed to protect us from the groundless abyss below our feet and to connect us to our neighbors becomes an increasingly dense veil made from science and art, philosophy and religion . . . so that we forget our solitude and death, including the death of the others whom we love." It thus functions as a veil that stops us from realizing our bottomless and absurd situation.

Flusser's view of communication as the forgetting of death is linked with the Jewish notion of remembering others to keep them alive. Our dead loved ones will continue to exist only as long as we remember them in our thoughts and daily conversations. On Flusser's gravestone in the New Jewish Cemetery in Prague, a verse from Hosea (14:10), printed together with a short Portuguese text, reads, *"Eu morro, tu morres, não morreremos"* (I will die, you will die, we will not die), implying that although we die alone, we survive together in the conversations of those still alive.

The second essential element of Flusser's communication theory is, therefore, the fundamentally dialogical intersubjective nature of all communication. We communicate with each other in the face of death and annihilation. Man is a *zoon politikon,* a political animal, as Aristotle put it, "not because he is a social animal, but because he is a solitary animal who cannot live in solitude." This perspective, as we shall see shortly, is also of great methodological importance for the elaboration of Flusser's communication theory.

Because of the inescapable existential dimension of all communication acts, a communication theory is above all a human science and not a natural science. Communication theory, according to Flusser, is not about explaining but about interpreting. He emphasizes, "If one tries to explain human communication" as a "particular method of transferring information . . . as opposed to trying to interpret it (indicating what it means), then one has a different sort of phenomenon in mind. . . . As a result 'communication theory' is understood as an interpretive discipline (for instance, in contrast to 'information theory' or 'information sciences'), and human communication is seen to be a meaningful phenomenon that must be interpreted." The decisive issue here is the deliberate choice of a specific perspective, in the Nietzschean sense, and the intentional relation of subject to object understood in a phenomenological, Husserlian sense. Each perspective calls for a different framing of the subject and highlights specific aspects instead of others. Communication is not about safe data transfer but about intentional acts of freedom.

Communication as Negentropy

In the closing section of his essay, Flusser expands the scope of his definition by connecting the individual side of communication, the microcosm, with the global aspect, the macrocosm, creating a fundamental link between the two. Philosophy is about translating, a pontifical task building bridges between that which is separate, in this case, the sublunar and the superlunar dimensions—to use Aristotle's words—which have undeniably fallen apart with the formulation of quantum theory in the early twentieth century. The search for a unified theory underlying all natural phenomena is ongoing. Even string theory, the most probable candidate, has been recently questioned as unscientific.

Human communication—and this presents Flusser's third fundamental aspect—is an attempt to negate death by accumulating information, that is, by the collective intentional production of different forms of codes:

> The artificiality of this phenomenon becomes apparent when viewed from the perspective of interpretation. The artificiality of its methods . . . is only part of the problem. Human communication is unnatural. In fact, it is perverse because it wants to store the information it acquires. It is "negatively entropic." One can assume that the transfer of acquired information from generation to generation is an essential aspect of human communication, a general characteristic of humankind: man is an animal that has discovered certain tricks for the purpose of storing acquired information. (*KO,* 12)

From the perspective of the natural sciences, the accumulation of information throughout human history appears a pretty hopeless affair, in view of the general entropic tendency of nature; but from an existential point of view, it becomes absolutely essential. As Flusser describes it,

> The storage of information is a process that, so to speak, plays itself out as an epicycle on top of a much larger process toward information loss. Eventually, it is absorbed by the larger process. The oak is more complex than the acorn; but it will eventually be reduced to ashes. . . . If one interprets the negentropic tendency of human communication instead of trying to explain it, then it appears in a different light. In this case, the accumulation of information is not seen as a process that is statistically improbable but possible. Rather, it seems as a human intention—not as a result of accident and necessity, but freedom. (*KO,* 12–13)

The word *epicycle* appears again and again in Flusser's work. It symbolizes two moments as it recalls the metaphor of the spiral and the circle we already came across in chapter 3. Instead of the straight line that Flusser critically associates with a highly problematic view of history as continuous growth and unchecked linear progress—or to use a term already mentioned, as the development of thought voraciously and aggressively conquering and assimilating reality—the circle and spiral represent a cyclical view, based on repetition and difference, corresponding in Flusser's work to the term *reflection,* thereby implying a self-critical backward movement. Uniform circular motion and epicycles were cataloged by Ptolemy in 150 A.D. They were used to account for the detailed motion of the planets on the celestial sphere when they moved around the earth. Although both circles actually rotate the same way, that is, counterclockwise, Flusser uses the concept to suggest the opposite. The bigger circle of cosmic entropy rotates one way, whereas the much smaller negentropic effort of mankind turns the other way. It contradicts, thus, the overall trend, but as it is carried by the larger circle, the effort is ultimately doomed to failure.

Just as Flusser's early translation theory served as an attempt to reunite the two main strands of philosophy, his communication theory tries to define the human condition in existential *and* cosmic terms, joining macro- and microcosm. Referring to the second law of thermodynamics and postulating the universal law of increasing entropy, he suggests that

> the storage of acquired information is not an exception to the law of thermodynamics (such as in information sciences), but rather, it is the perverse intention of a human being condemned to death. . . . The thesis that human communication is an artistic technique against the solitude unto death . . . and the thesis that human communication is a process directed

against the general entropic tendency of "nature" [are one and the same]. The impassive tendency of nature to move toward more probable conditions . . . toward ashes (toward "heat death"), is nothing more than the objective corollary of the subjective experience of our own stultifying solitude and condemnation to death. Viewed from an existential perspective . . . or from a formal perspective . . . , human communication seems to be an attempt to deny nature. This denial is concerned not only with "nature" out there, but also with human "nature." (*KO*, 13)

Dialogue and Discourse

Flusser distinguishes between two contrary but complementary intersubjective principles: dialogue and discourse. Neither dialogue nor discourse can exist on its own. The difference between the two is a matter of perspective; that is, it depends on the position of the viewer and his distance to the subject. The two principles presuppose and are dependent on each other. Dialogues are necessary to create new information by recombining already existing information. New information, on the other hand, is stored in discourses whose aim it is to conserve and transmit it to future generations. No dialogue is possible if there is no previous information available. And conversely, there can be no discourse without the production of new information to be stored. To ask oneself which of the two comes first is devoid of meaning. It is like asking which came first: the chicken or the egg?

The ideal form of a relationship between the two principles is a perfect balance. This gives us a perspective on history insofar as certain periods were more dialogical or discursive than others. Flusser tries, thus, to explain specific historical settings by the predominant way of communication, similar to Marshall McLuhan. This perspective, although in a way very original, suffers from reductionism by circumscribing the complexity of specific historical periods to a monocausal explanation: the prevailing communicative asset. Two complementary examples taken from Flusser himself will illustrate the idea. The prerevolutionary period in France at the end of the eighteenth century was primarily dialogical, that is, dominated by round tables, commissions, discussion groups, and *assemblées constitutionelles*. The more nationalistic and conservative German romantic movement, on the other hand, flowering only a few decades later, was above all discursive and clearly favored public speakers.

Each dialogue can be considered as a series of discourses, and each discourse can be seen as part of a dialogue. A book of philosophy, for instance, taken on its own, may be considered a discourse because it contains a set of information ready to be used. Together with other books of its kind, however, it becomes a dialogue, revealing its fundamentally intertextual nature. Moving still further away, these very books join together to form a specific discourse, the discourse of Western philosophy, for example. So every time we zoom out or zoom in, the situation changes, switching from dialogue to discourse and back again.

Although the two principles of dialogue and discourse are inseparable, the difference between them is absolute, and the consequences for those that engage in them are radically different. Flusser discusses this point in *Kommunikologie* with an ironic reference to the present situation. Although written in the mid-1970s, his commentary is all the more poignant today in view of the global success of cellular phones and satellite TV. We keep lamenting the difficulties we have in communicating with each other, writes Flusser, probably referring to a theme also very popular in the *Absurd Drama* of Ionesco and in Beckett of the late 1960s. What this implies, however, is not so much the lamented absence of communication but the difficulty to create truly new dialogues. In fact, never before have there been so many ways and means of communication. Where does the difficulty come from then? Flusser describes it as a lack of equilibrium between dialogue and discourse, if you want, a sort of dysfunction. "We can explain this difficulty," proposes Flusser in *Kommunikologie*, "by examining the present day perfection in the functioning of communication, thanks to the unparalleled omnipresence of discourses that make any dialogue impossible and unnecessary" (*KO*, 17). Our period, then, is characterized by a predominance of extremely effective discourses in conjunction with archaic and insufficient forms of dialogue. In other words, conservation and distribution prevail over production and creativity.

Communication Structures

Starting from this initial division of discourse and dialogue, Flusser works out a series of abstract settings of communication, four predominantly discursive and two predominantly dialogical. At the same time, he uses his description of communicative models to recount the history of Western civilization moving from tribal and nomadic societies to sedentary power structures, from religion to science, and from archaic to highly sophisticated means of communication. Although abstract models, each of the six structures can easily be demonstrated by a concrete historical example. Let us begin with the four discourse structures.

Two major problems within these communicative structures are fidelity and progression. Fidelity is necessary to stop noises from altering the information to be transmitted, keeping them as they were first intended. Flusser is probably thinking here of the fidelity of the translator to the original text. Progression, on the other hand, ensures the success of discourse by transforming its receivers into future senders. Only in this way can information, safely stored, be carried over into new historical contexts to serve as a starting point for new creative dialogues.

Discourses, thus, are in themselves ambiguous in that they possess a conservative and preserving dimension as well as a dynamic potential of innovation. "These two aspects," insists Flusser in *Kommunikologie,* "are problematic because, in a certain sense, they contradict each other. 'Fidelity' to the information and 'progression' of the information are difficult to reconcile" (*KO,* 20). The real challenge is to conceive of a communicative structure capable of doing both. This remains not so much a question of input and output, as information theory would have it. From the intersubjective point of view Flusser has taken up, it becomes a radically political question, a question of intention and decision.

Theaters

The first model is theatrical-discourse. It consists of a concave wall behind a sender standing in front of a limited group of receivers. Flusser uses the vocabulary of information theory throughout, combining it with his intersubjective approach that is peppered with a strong sensibility for wordplay and metaphorical thinking. The result is a slightly ironic hybrid in tune with Flusser's overall attitude toward philosophy and theoretical construction. The aforementioned concept of progression (in German, *Fortschritt*), for instance, literally means "moving forward" but, at the same time, "progress" in the historical sense. Flusser very often plays at the limits of literal and figurative meaning, mostly in a critical attempt to retranslate the abstract concept into the concreteness of a gesture—to put it another way, to point out the hidden metaphoric dimension of concepts by exposing their pictorial content. But let us return to theatrical-discourse.

Flusser uses the structure of the classical theater of antiquity to make his point: in this discourse, the receiver can immediately react to the messages of the sender. In this sense, she is directly involved in what is going on; in short, she is in a responsible position. She can even stand up, storm the scene, turn to the public, and address it. Flusser calls this a "revolution," implying again a double, political, and literal meaning—the gesture of revolving, the transformation of spectator into actor, of student into teacher. The weak spot of this structure is, of course, fidelity, not progression.

Pyramids

The second discursive structure of communication, the pyramid, presents an attempt to solve this problem by creating an original sender—author, authority, and collective memory. The message is sent down a hierarchical structure. To make sure that the original information remains unchanged, a series of relays have been added to the structure. Their aim is to check the validity of the incoming message, cleansing it of any possible interference or noise. From a certain point on, there is no longer any possibility of double-checking the information with its original form. It simply flows down unchecked to the lowest levels of society. One is, of course, immediately reminded of armies, churches, political parties, and theocratic societies such as the Egyptian pharaohs. Pyramids are a solution to the problem of fidelity, but of course, within this system, responsibility or revolution are no longer possible.

Trees

To conserve the undeniable advantages of pyramidal discourses while eliminating their disadvantages, tree-structures developed. At this point, one is tempted to probe, how do these changes come about? Are they the result of the intervention of concrete people? Flusser's description suggests that the process itself is governed by an inner logic of trial and error. Each new stage is an answer to a preexisting problem, but at the same time, it is also the cause of a new problem, calling for another solution.

The actual historical subject in a Marxist sense seems to disappear behind the relentless unfolding of an initial conflict, a cleft, always asking for a new solution that quickly turns out to create an additional problem. As we shall see shortly, the same logic directs the inherent dialectics of image and text. Let us go back to the tree-structure.

Two fundamental changes become apparent: the crossing of the channels and the elimination of a final receiver. The top of the structure, furthermore, is no longer a clearly recognizable authority but a forgotten empty source. Trees are to be found in universities and other academic groupings. The original information is progressively recoded and deconstructed, leading to an endless production of new information. We assist in an explosive development of diversification, leading to more and more hermetic codes accessible to smaller and smaller audiences. This way, the actual receiver disappears. The explosive and hermetic nature of this discourse has ensured its enormous success, but the price to be paid for this was its ultimate insignificance for a wider audience. Information has turned inhuman. This crisis calls for a new development.

Amphitheaters

"To avoid the growing danger inherent in the specialization of information distribution," Flusser continues in *Kommunikologie*, that is putting at risk "the very aim of human communication"—prevailing over the solitude onto death—a fourth communicative structure comes into being (*KO,* 26). The amphitheatrical structure is a development of its predecessor, the theatrical structure, and is slowly taking its place. As the name itself already suggests, Flusser is thinking here of the circus, in particular, the coliseum during the Roman Empire, that operated as a safety valve within a highly controversial political setting—*panem et circenses*: amusement to appease the populace. As shall become clear later on, Flusser draws parallels to present-day mass media, above all, television.

Contrary to the theater, this structure is characterized by a cosmic openness and a complete absence of frontiers, as the protective wall in the back has been disposed. It consists of two elements only: a sender suspended in empty space and programmed with all the necessary information to be distributed and a series of channels through which to transport it. The receivers are present in the form of dust afloat in the limitless space around the central sender. They are memories programmed, gauged, to receive certain channels to be programmed by them. The complete absence of any clearly recognizable structure in the masses out there to be programmed is entirely intentional. The receivers can only receive but are unable to become senders themselves. They are isolated consumers without any contact with each other, as Günther Anders would have put it. In this situation, revolution as well as responsibility has become utterly impossible. The hermetic, specializing codification of the tree-structures has been happily overcome by a universalizing, uniform(ing) code. The senders can send forever; in this sense, they are truly immortal. They can go on sending even after all receivers have disappeared. The implicit irony pervading the text becomes apparent when Flusser concludes that this form of communication is the most perfectly suited for distribution. "It is a communicative perfection that in other contexts would receive the name of 'totalitarianism'" (*KO*, 28).

Flusser has compared the world of modern mass media not only to imperial Rome but also to the Baroque period. In *Nachgeschichte* [Posthistory], published in the early 1980s, Flusser muses, "We possess the same dismal Rationalism—for instance logic, cybernetics, informatics—and the same in reverse, the same witchcraft irrationalism—for instance mass-media. We are also Counter-Reformatory" (*PH,* 11). Globalization is therefore to be seen as a form of pseudoreligious recolonization of the planet.

Circles and Nets

Dialogues, as we have seen, synthesize new information from already existing dialogues. The novelty consists in the originality of the combination. Flusser distinguishes between two crucial dialogical communication structures: the circle and the net. In contrast to the discursive structures, no historical development is intended here as the two forms possess an archaic as well as a very modern dimension. Examples for circular-dialogues are round tables, committees, parliaments, and campfires. Their structure is of enormous simplicity but also of great effectiveness. People sit around a central point. This circularity ensures that everybody can look at everybody else and abolishes hierarchical differences by placing everybody on the same level. Round tables are, consequently, more democratic than square tables. The problem of this structure is that it is basically a closed circuit, limiting the number of people taking part by defining criteria of acceptance. Circular-dialogues are an excellent form when it comes to making decisions, but their nature remains elitist and therefore antidemocratic.

Net-dialogues differ from their circular counterpart by being open circuits through which any kind of information can travel freely. This openness, however, is at the same time its crucial flaw. Net-dialogues absorb everything—conversations, discussions, hearsay, gossip, rumor, idle talk—without making any qualitative distinctions. "This diffuse form of communication," proposes Flusser, "forms the primary net *(reseau fondamental),* on which all other forms of communication are based, soaking up all information elaborated by man" (*KO,* 32). The postal system and the telephone system are examples of this kind of communication, but so are the Internet with its chat lines and blogs and the global net of cellular phones. In this context, information is not produced through conscientious and selective discussion, as in the circular structure; rather, it develops spontaneously through deformation of the available information by noise. Flusser compares it to the public opinion or its medieval version, vox populi. Net-dialogues are a reservoir in which all existing information accumulates. Although fundamentally democratic, in the populist sense of grassroots democracy, insofar as anybody can take part in them, they are also subject to entropy.

Synchronizations

Flusser ends his analysis with a description of the present situation, which, in the early 1970s when he was writing, seemed nothing short of prophetic. Theatrical-discourse and circular-dialogues have entered a profound crisis. It is a crisis of ethical and political nature—of responsibility and revolution, as Flusser calls it—directly affecting human relationships. Pyramidal authoritarian discourse is still an important form of communication, even if it has lost its former grip on people's minds. The present revival of religious fundamentalism and political conservatism seems to contradict Flusser's prophecy here. Tree-structures (scientific and technological discourse) hold sway: the recent technological revolution of new media has definitely confirmed Flusser's prophetic appraisal. The process even accelerated considerably in the last few years. Scientific terminology, along with the behavior it evinces, has overwhelmed everyday life in the last two decades. "Our situation," surmises Flusser, is determined by "a synchronization of technically highly evolved amphitheatrical-discourses along with net-dialogues that have remained still very archaic but can always be improved—

complete de-politicization with apparent global participation" (*KO,* 34). As both net-dialogues and amphitheatrical-discourses function along the same lines, this synchronization produces a complete lack of any sense of responsibility toward the circulating information. An example could be the way in which reality shows on TV or the private lives of stars and celebrities invade and occupy everyday conversation. This phenomenon, observes Flusser, is well known from antiquity: "The present day concurrence of amphitheater and net, of mass-media and consensus, however, is unparalleled. Our amphitheater is not the continuation of theatrical-discourse, but an extension of the tree-structure of science and technology, and our consensus is not the world-wide diffusion of the original village-chatter, but a form of turning banal and sensationalizing the distributed information that can be scientifically and technically manipulated" (*KO,* 48). There is, so to speak, difference in continuity. We will come across the same kind of consideration when dealing with technical images. *In fact,* they do look like traditional pictures, but they are *in fact* the product of scientific programs.

In light of the gravity of the present situation—which Flusser at a certain point defines as apocalyptical—the political task at hand would be to stop random noise from affecting net-dialogues and to start informing them with a sense of responsibility. To achieve this, Flusser proposes a countersynchronization of net-dialogues with theatrical-discourse: "Theatrical-discourse is the only known form of communication allowing for responsible participation in the conservation of information and its distribution to future generations. And the circular-dialogue is the only known form of communication that allows conscious participation in the dissemination of new information and in decision making" (*KO,* 36).

Media Theory

In Flusser's view, every aspect of reality is mediated, which leads him to neglect the meaning of the notion of medium. As a consequence, the concept has not been explored as systematically as the idea of communication. Flusser is not really interested in media. His understanding of them is unclear, shifting, sometimes contradictory, and basically critical. What he deals with in his writings are dialogical and discursive communication structures and the codes that operate within them. He therefore neglects the mediatic presuppositions of codes. Even in his numerous essays on the functioning of the telephone, the television set, and the camera, he does not give us any analysis of their hardware. Gadgets do not play any role in his communication and media theory.

At least four different media concepts can be detected in his work. First of all, media are described as communication structures. These operate the way syntax does, that is, by organizing content. The codes that function within them—the content—are seen as the semantic side of the phenomenon. Mass media, especially television, are considered to be uncritical and ideological because they are not dialogical. Media are also used in the sense of signs or codes. Languages, as well as texts and pictures, are media. And finally, media mediate between humans and their environment, and by doing this, they connect and separate at the same time. This, as we will see later on, is also true of codes. But let us introduce a few examples to render this paradoxical dimension of media a bit clearer. A round table connects the people sitting around it, but it also stands between them, separating them from each other. The same would be true of a window. It allows us to contemplate the outside world, but it frames and separates us from it. To sum up, Flusser uses the concept of medium in several different and contradictory ways, allowing for contaminations between the concepts of medium and code as well as medium and communication structure.

Another reason for Flusser's deep mistrust of the media concept originates in his criticism of the work of Marshall McLuhan, whose theoretical achievements are of great importance for Flusser's own communication and media theory. One might even say that Flusser developed most of it by clearly distancing himself from McLuhan's work. For Flusser, "the medium is not the message": "the function of codes," insists Flusser in *Kommunikologie*, "does not depend on the metaphysical *eidos* of the medium (as McLuhan is inclined to think) but on the way the medium is used" (*KO*, 272). Media do not possess any one-sided structural trait wired into their hardware and independent of their concrete use within a given sociopolitical setting. As Flusser put it further down, "McLuhan is wrong with his assumption that amphitheatrical media, like the press or TV, can transform the world into a cosmic village: they will transform it into a cosmic circus" (*KO*, 274). Only a radical change in their use, a dialogical replugging, can avoid a cultural catastrophe. The amphitheatrical senders do not hide any socially autonomous mythical principle but, as Flusser explains, "the intention to provoke in all accessible receivers a certain kind of behavior by irradiating a message" (*KO*, 284).

Codes

Essential changes in human history do not come about because of the invention of new technologies or media but because of fundamental changes in the predominant code. "The overthrow of codes," claims Flusser, "brought about by neural simulation emanating from TVs, computers and video, is at least as extraordinary as the overthrow caused by the steam-engine" (*KO*, 236). Codes are defined as systems of symbols. Their purpose is to make communication between humans possible. Because symbols are phenomena representing other phenomena, communication is always a form of substitution. Codes, the two essential ones for Flusser being images and texts, were invented to describe the reality for which they stand. As such, they are subject to the dialectical tension of all media. They start out by representing a certain reality and end up taking its place.

Apparatus

Flusser neglects media as gadgets and the hardware question to avoid a purely technological perspective. When describing the functioning of the camera or any other gadget, Flusser always opts for the anthropological, that is, intersubjective dimension, the way media change our being-in-the-world. The relevant questions consequently are, what is the gesture of photographing or filmmaking? What are their philosophical implications? In which way do they alter our relation to the world and to others?

The idea of media is, for Flusser, furthermore linked with the concept of the apparatus, which carries ambiguous, if not openly negative, connotations. Auschwitz was a dehumanizing apparatus in which people functioned in view of an overall destructive aim. But also the photographic camera can be seen as an apparatus, a black box within which a series of transformations takes place. The apparatus can also be seen as a complex toy simulating thought. Its complexity is so high that the person playing with it cannot fully understand it. This is one of its salient characteristics. Some fully automated apparatuses work on their own—some computers, for instance—whereas others require human intervention. The human appendage of the apparatus, the player or functionary, can control its functioning by regulating the input and the output, but he cannot change its programs. Functionaries can function according to the rules of the apparatus. People working in concentration camps or within an inscrutable labyrinthine, Kafkaesque administration complex are examples of this basically dehumanizing side of apparatuses. They give their freedom and responsibility over to the system. But one can also work against the apparatus by trying to bend and alter its program to attain new results. This is the case of the photographer who plays with the camera to create unexpected, surprising pictures.

Image and Text

In Vilém Flusser's work, codes and media operate in McLuhan's sense as translators and trans-coders. Images transpose reality into situations. Writing transfers the circular magical time of pictures into the time of linear history. The photographic camera translates history into programs.

In *Toward a Philosophy of Photography,* first published in English in 1984, Flusser develops a history of media based on a series of processes of translation and retranslation. These transformations take place between two essential codes: images and texts. Flusser defines images as significant surfaces obtained by reducing the primary four-dimensional human experience—three-dimensional space plus time—to the two dimensions of the plane. Images were invented to render the world out there imaginable, that is, understandable to us *(vorstellen)*. Texts, on the other hand, are one-dimensional codes obtained by placing single letters and words on lines.

In a "Lexicon of Basic Concepts" at the end of the book, *translating* is defined as a "move from code to code," a "jump from one universe into another" (PP, 61). The first step in this evolutionary process, based on an alternation of images and texts, consists in the creation of surfaces whose function is to make the world imaginable by abstracting it. These surfaces were meant to be mediations between humans and the world but tended to hide *(verstellen)* the world by slowly absorbing and substituting it. "The world becomes image-like," writes Flusser, and he continues, "This reversal of the function of images may be called 'idolatry'" (PP, 7). To counteract this tendency, texts were invented. Their aim was to break up the hallucinatory relationship of humans to the image and to criticize imagination by recalling its original intention. Flusser explains, "Some men . . . attempted to destroy the screen in order to open the way to the world again. Their method was to tear the image elements out from the surface and to align them. They invented linear writing. In doing so, they transcoded the circular time of magic into the linear time of history" (PP, 7). History, as Flusser writes, can thus be defined as the "progressive translation of ideas into concepts," of images into texts (PP, 60).

The dialectics of mediation at work in the passage from the first to the second step of evolution, however, leads to a second impasse. "The purpose of writing," states Flusser, "is to mediate between man and his images, to explain them. In doing so, texts interpose themselves between man and image: they hide the world from man instead of making it transparent for him. . . . Texts grow unimaginable, and man lives as a function of his texts. A 'textolatry' occurs, which is just as hallucinatory as idolatry" (PP, 9).

In the same way the prehistoric phase of images was overtaken by a historical phase of texts, posthistory takes over from history and, by inventing technical images, attempts to make texts imaginable again. By doing so, posthistory bends the progressive linear development of translation from images into texts back to its origins and beyond. Flusser describes this process as a "re-translation of concepts into ideas," that is, of texts into technical images (PP, 61). Technical images differ from traditional images in that the two are the result of dissimilar processes of translation. Traditional images have real situations as their source; technical images, on the other hand, start out from texts, which in turn have been written to break up images through translation, that is, images containing texts with images in their belly. "The present situation," analyzes Flusser in "Line and Surface," published in the volume *Writings,* "does not look like the result of a linear development from image to concept, but rather like the result of a sort of spiral movement from image through concept to image."[1]

If one tries to draw an analogy between Flusser's earlier history of communication structures and his later history of media evolution, a few correspondences emerge, showing again how his work grows by constant cogitation and self-cannibalistic rumination. Two examples shall illustrate this. The invention of technical images coincides with the crises of tree-structures—because of their hermetic, inhuman aspect—and the invention of technically advanced amphitheatrical-discourses. In fact, the universalizing tendency of modern mass media culture is achieved through the distribution of technical images. The idea of a possible utopian equilibrium between discourse and dialogue represents itself as a balance between images and texts. If, in the first case, the ideal seems to Flusser to have been nearly attained in democratic Greece, the second aspect is associated with Leonardo da Vinci's *fantasia essata.* Leonardo's universalistic aspirations on the border of art and philosophy, science and technology, find their truest expression in a sort of phenomenological science in which concepts are related to images of scenes and not abstract notions of reality.

Telematic Society

In his work on Walter Benjamin's essay "The Task of the Translator," Andrew Benjamin refers to the concept of *tikkun,* which is of great interest in view of Flusser's own messianic vision of history as a translational process. This myth postulates the reestablishment of a harmonious condition of the world, a reconstitution that is to be understood as an initial constitution. This plan does not, however, imply the idea of "the retrieval of the past, but rather a futural projection."[2] Instead of espousing the biblical view of an initial language fragmented in many individual languages after the fall of the tower of Babel, the Kabbalah posits the idea of a basic multiplicity of languages, claiming that it is not the result of a sinful action. The fragmentation of this original vessel does not refer to the lost unity of a sound initial vessel. It points, rather, as Andrew Benjamin continues, to "the possibility of unity and totality in which the parts of the vessel remain as parts but within a generalised belonging together. Fundamental to such a totality is the presence of difference (involving) a harmony which is the belonging together of differences."[3] This remark also holds true for Flusser's own vision of translation, not only insofar as the status of the final version of his (re)-translation practice is concerned but also in view of his philosophy of history.

The very last translational jump in his history of media evolution, as we have seen, carries us back to the very beginning, but, and this is an essential feature of all retranslational moves, it carries us onto a radically new level. It brings about a new sense of concreteness, not the four-dimensional concreteness of the beginning from which humans separated themselves and started through the series of evolutionary jumps.

It is a secondary concreteness, reminiscent of Heinrich von Kleist's short philosophical essay "On the Marionette Theater," written in 1810. The text, conceived as a simulated dialogue, sets out with a discussion about marionettes, ending up in a reflection on the nature of man as an alienated being, forever separated from the reality in which he lives. Man has eaten from the tree of knowledge and thus acquired consciousness. Our capacity for reflection and self-consciousness, our being humans, however, prevent us from acting with the instinctual simplicity of an animal. There is no way back to the Garden of Eden. We are doomed to perennial exile. Humankind will never coincide with itself or the world in which it lives. The only way out of this dilemma is to go back all the way through the Garden of Eden in the hope that it possibly opens up on the other side, leading us into a world of complete self-awareness. We may eventually be able to carry out the actions we choose with the same confidence and harmony as a marionette dancing on the strings of a puppeteer. Because of the initial split, we are neither gods nor animals. There is hope, however, that we might bring the two sides together again. Human history, then, is played out between complete forgetting and absolute knowledge.

Flusser's history of media evolution is conceived of as a series of disappointments, a history of growing disillusionment with respect to the ability of media to mediate between humans and reality. Each new code promises in the beginning to set us free from the predominance of the earlier one, only to become predominant in its own turn. With the last stage, however, the process finally seems to come to an end, definitively abolishing the duality of humans and reality and substituting for it a completely and consciously man-made world of absolute artificiality projected onto the screen of nothingness that surrounds us. There is no "world out there" anymore. We only meet the codes we have dialogically created ourselves and recognize them fully as the outcome of our own collective achievement.

Flusser captures this development in *Ins Universum der technischen Bilder* [Into the Universe of Technical Images], first published in 1985, in a downward series of numbers, as a sort of ironic countdown: 4–3–2–1–0. The numbers indicate spatial dimensions and are linked to specific codes as well as parts of the body determining our interaction with reality. On the first, four-dimensional level, the moment of concrete experience, man, who is not really man yet, is completely surrounded by an environment in which he bathes. The next, three-dimensional level is dominated by the hands grabbing things and changing them. The eyes linked to the birth of two-dimensional pictures determine the pictorial stage. The fingers are associated with the one-dimensional linear universe of texts. And finally, the fingertips belong to the zero-dimensional world of calculated and computed technical images, a world of discreet numbers, dots, bits, and pixels. Flusser's zero-dimension is reminiscent of other similar conceptions, of Roland Barthes's *le degré zero de l'écriture* or Merleau-Ponty's degree zero of being; it forms a precondition of a new society and a new Adamic world in the kabbalistic, messianic sense of the word, a world in which the human is author and reader of the reality of her own myths and constructions.

6 | Science as Fiction, Fiction as Science

The word *fiction* contains largely positive connotations when it appears in a literary or artistic context. The same word, however, continues to conjure up rather negative associations when it is understood as the antithesis of reality. Regardless, these two perspectives mix and blur. During the eighteenth and especially the nineteenth centuries, consuming fictional works was considered a problem, as a world of dangerous illusions could capture the reader. The word *fiction* may also be used in scientific contexts. Scientific experiments fail to access certain experiences and areas of reality, either directly or at any time. Such phenomena may only be captured hypothetically. Moreover, the scientific hypothesis itself presents a form of deductive fiction. The physicist, for example, realizes his experiment using movement by excluding gravity or aerodynamic resistance: an exercise in fictional thinking. The poet experiences fiction as raw material from which she creates her own truth; the scientist, in contrast, plays with it as an instrument that facilitates the approach toward a truth.

Flusser traverses all these ideas and connotations in the attempt to understand how we think, what we think, and why.

To think the world at all, we need to invent or reconstruct it by means of diverse fictions. In an unpublished letter to Maria L. Leão from 1983, he writes, "I share the distrust towards analogies . . . however, we would not comprehend anything without using models."[1]

Flusserian Fiction

In his essay "Da ficção"[2] [Of Fiction], Flusser enumerates a range of assorted imaginations according to which the world is similar to deceptive fiction. The Platonists insisted that we merely perceive shadows; medieval Christianity thought of the world as a nightmare invented by the devil; during the Renaissance, humankind viewed the world as a dream, whereas in Baroque times, it was considered a stage; finally, during romanticism, the world appeared to constitute subjective representation. The fictive character of the world and hence of reality presents cause for lament in all these cases. Nonetheless, for Flusser, all imaginations listed earlier are appropriate; however, he questions the dismissive standpoints accompanying them. According to Flusser, we have to acknowledge the fictive character of the world, but we should not complain about it. Several apocalyptic philosophers—among them Jean Baudrillard—maintain that the sign has absorbed the signifier, making the former more real than reality: in some sort of diabolical fashion, the simulacrum has transformed reality to become its shadow. Flusser emphatically disagrees with this perspective and observes that the known world has always existed as a simulacrum and that reality as a whole cannot be ascertained.

The virtual does not stand in opposition to reality but to an ideal of truth. The world as such is not a fiction, but the ensemble of ideational conceptualizations with which we are aiming to understand it is. We encounter illusions everywhere: as an ideal of truth or as the illusion about the end of all illusions. The dissatisfactory evaluation we have come to associate with the idea of the simulacrum points to a long tradition reaching as far back as Plato. Likewise, one's proverbial common sense considers every illusion a lie, even if it concerns the make-believe of a magician, fooleries, or fictitious narratives. Science, phenomenology, and cybernetics, on the other hand, acknowledge the impossibility of recognizing exhaustively the world's fleeting appearances that can only be reconstructed by means of hypotheses and fictive designs. Whoever reproduces a phenomenon or object with the aid of a simulacrum or model merely identifies its partial elements—because every model, just as every metaphor, highlights certain characteristics while eclipsing others—but she learns something essential about it as well.

We would like to consult Flusser's example from his essay "Da ficção" to clarify what has been said so far. Is the table at which the reader is sitting real, or is it simply the fiction of a table? Although it may be a solid table that holds other books as well, Flusser points out that this idea is a fiction we can describe as the "reality of the senses." Another point of view determines the table as an almost empty electromagnetic and gravitational field underneath other, equivalent and fluctuating fields called "books." But this, too, is a fiction. We call it the "reality of exact science." From the perspective of physics, the table appears to be solid, but in reality, it is empty. From the perspective of our senses, however, the table appears to be empty, but in reality, it is solid. Does the table, therefore, consist of two different fictions? According to Flusser, this is a meaningless question because, abstractly speaking, no one perspective can ultimately be more truthful than another. In actuality, every perspective enriches all others; the diverse fictions complement each other without diametrically opposing one another.

This scientific explanation does not necessarily contradict our everyday perception; it merely refines it. One perspective, in this sense, does not lay claim to more truth than another; however, more often than not, it is more appropriate, more productive, or more credible. Problematic situations do not evolve until we select a particular fiction as the only truth and when we begin to negate all other perspectives. We face another problem in that we avoid suspicion directed at our own models of reality by quickly replacing a reality that has become questionable with the subject. Flusser contradicts the viewpoints of both the realists and the idealists: the absence of a perceiving subject invalidates the object, and the absence of a perceived object annuls the subject—it is nothing. Reality can be located neither in the object nor in the subject alone, but in their interrelationship. Tables and subjects are abstractions; their interrelationships, however, are concrete.

Such argumentation leads us into the area of modern relativism. It is dangerous to argue for the relativity and equivalence of all kinds of perspectives because such simplification facilitates a position of "anything goes." If everything were relative, nothing could really be relative, simply because things are always relative to something else, and that, in return, has to be deemed absolute at the relational moment. Even Einstein's theory of relativity eagerly determined what remained absolute: in that case, the speed of light. Relativist considerations are necessary, of course, yet they merely present a first step. We have to continue with our thoughts, that is, our doubts, because if we agree that everything is relative, we interrupt our thought process halfway. For this reason, Flusser asks, would it be feasible to remove all possible perspectives so that in the end we would be left with something approximating the essence of the object? Flusserian phenomenology would say that even then, the essence of the object would ultimately elude us. However, we could examine the intentionalities that would have become visible following a description of the object. Basically, for Flusser, the object consists of the sum of all perspectives a subject may take up vis-à-vis an object. In other words, the table is the ensemble of perspectives that provide its shape, the intersection of diverse fictions. If Flusserian phenomenology were capable of removing all these fictions just like skinning an onion, we would be left with what we find inside the onion: nothing. The image of the onion—applied to reality—argues that truth contains neither a core nor a center and that we cannot grasp any essence beyond appearances. Despite such findings, it remains necessary to peel away one layer of appearance after another, just like Sisyphus repeatedly rolls the stone uphill. We need to continue to think and research as if we could grasp the truth of things.

Pilpul

Flusser's interpretation of the term *Pilpul*—a "sophistic-playful method of studying the Talmud, developed in the 16th century" (*JS,* 139)—is pivotal in this context because it embodies simultaneously the idea of an elusive core and a multiperspectival, multilingual thought process repeatedly ignited by contradiction: "an incomplete and never to be completed circling" (*JS,* 149). If Western thought seeks to "render the unthinkable thinkable," Jewish thought, in contrast, seeks to identify contradictions "as unanswerable, as a sign of the limits of human thought. Jewish thought runs up against the borders of the thinkable, not in order to demolish them, but rather to ascertain them. I think that is Pilpul" (*JS,* 141). The specifically Jewish form of reflection, according to Flusser, "is a dance around a given object, it attacks the object from different vantage points, recedes in different directions only to approach it again and come upon other reflections. This dynamic of reflection, by the way, figures concretely on the Talmud page: the object in the middle of the page, the reflections in converging circles" (*JS,* 141). We can construe this from the page structure of the Babylonian Talmud to understand how nondiscursive, that is, nonlinear, thinking operates. "There is a word or several words in the middle of the page and a few textual circles loop concentrically around this core. We immediately see that this core is to be pondered . . . and the rotating circles contemplate the core (they are the 'commentary'). But this structure is far from easy: the circles do not only comment on the core, but also on each other. That is called Pilpul" (*JS*, 144). The rings that form in time, just like with a tree around its central core, were written by different authors at different moments in time and are multilingual, usually in Hebrew and Aramaic, two related languages: "Pilpul does not seek to affirm or negate the item to which we keep returning, but to approach it from as many standpoints as possible and to bring those into conflict with each other. It is as if Pilpul had switched over from a 'true–false' logic into a multiply rooted logic" (*JS*, 149–50).

The Principle of "As If"

We do not intrinsically approach reality via things; we approach it via relationships generated through things. Because such relationships are constructed similarly to fictions, we should closely examine the modalities determining our handling of fictions. Fictions are an "as if." The author invents fictions posing as realities, and the reader encounters them as if they represented the most truthful of truths. Indeed, reading a fictional text can be so powerful that the act may appear more real than immediate reality. We read the text as if it were true and as if we—in the process of reading—had become someone else who claims just as much reality, if not more, as our everyday *I*.

The concept "as if," of course, is significant for the theory of fiction as well as philosophy. The neo-Kantian Hans Vaihinger coined the term in his 1911 *The Philosophy of "As If,"* a text Flusser already mentions in *Língua e realidade* (*LR,* 206) and that influenced Flusser greatly. Vaihinger posited that we describe as fictions the theoretical requirements guiding our practice. Fictions enable a partial grasp of reality, but they do not claim to comprehend it as a whole. In chapter 20, titled "The Separation of Scientific from Other Fictions, Particularly from the Aesthetic," Vaihinger seeks to distinguish various fictions: scientific fictions, according to Vaihinger, do not comprise the novels of Jules Verne; rather they represent an ensemble of scientifically produced fictions to facilitate an approximate calculation of reality. He suggests that we designate all scientific models as fictions and assigns the concept figment to mythological and aesthetic models. For example, the atom would be a fiction; the winged horse Pegasus, however, would be a figment. Additionally, he points out that *fictio* contains a secondary notion, rendering the concept significant in a pragmatic sense as well: the word *fiction* juristically represents practical expedience, that is, a fiction functions as a means to attune reality to particular research goals.

Vaihinger's conception of truth refers back to Nietzsche's essay *On Truth and Lie in an Extra-moral Sense*: "What then is truth? A mobile army of metaphors, metonyms, and anthropomorphisms—in short, a sum of human relations, which have been enhanced, transposed, and embellished poetically and rhetorically, and which after long use seem firm, canonical, and obligatory to a people: truths are illusions about which one has forgotten that is what they are."[3] In other words, truth and fiction are primarily phenomena of language. However, this does not imply that nothing cannot be true anymore; on the contrary, we as (re)-searchers are responsible for all truths we produce. "All these ideas," Vaihinger continues, "are not images of an event, they are themselves an event, a part of the cosmic event."[4] The world of representations is not a straightforward reflection of reality; it is an instrument that helps to simplify our orientation in the world.

Yet when fictions represent the world they simultaneously create other worlds, possibly leading to inner conflicts, which, in turn, generate paradoxes. We should not negate or explain away such conflicts because they display a thought process. Here Descartes would refer to crossing through moments of doubt and Nietzsche to truth as a multiplicity of metaphors. Vaihinger himself would describe this process of cognition as a path running through a territory obstructed by fictions, and Wittgenstein would alert us to the idea that thinking itself is limited by language. Which answer to this problem do we find in Flusser's oeuvre?

Mirror and Speculation

Flusser tried to formulate an original, independent synthesis of these different approaches, based on the concept of fiction. He supposed that each discourse was fictive and that precisely for that reason, the conditions of its fictionality had to be explicated. This applies particularly to philosophical discourse, most important, when it draws near poetry—invariably leading to conflict. Philosophers are concerned with concepts and court the concordance of word and thing. In the process, they reject the poetic. At least in academic and university circles, philosophy tends to prefer the precision and coherence of research to the vagueness of poetic thought. A philosophical poet and poetical philosopher such as Flusser chooses a different path: he is searching for a style of writing and thinking that can express his speculative position with the goal to develop and stimulate new ideas. In his essay "Do espelho"[5] [About the Mirror], he stresses that the word *speculation* is closely related to *mirror (speculum)* and that the mirror undeniably reflects reality but in inverted fashion. For that reason, everyone who reflects should be interested in the mirror. Abraham Moles named his essay about Flusser's *Vampyroteuthis infernalis,* titled "Flusser's Philosophical

Fiction," precisely for its speculative character: Moles believes that Flusser's particular style of writing reveals an entirely new way for different discourses to engage with each other. Flusser's hybrid metaphorical imagination and his method of perpetually changing positions present both "a philosophical adventure" and "a prime example of the phenomenological method." Indeed, "theoretical biology, phenomenology of perception, and logical analysis intersect right here."[6]

Gabriel Borba, Flusser's assistant in São Paulo, uses a particular metaphor to describe the metaphor of philosophical fiction.[7] Imagine a rug lying on the floor, and you use two fingers to pull it up at a particular point—where one pulls first is irrelevant. Depending on one's strength, the entire rug could be lifted up. Every minimal variation of the chosen point, however, creates considerable shifts, affecting the complete control of the rug and the creases that form in the process. We can compare Flusser's style of writing with the various attempts to pull up this imaginary rug: the assorted points at which we pull up the rug are dynamic, argument filled, and reflexive whirls that allow for remarkable rhetorical constructions. How does Flusser achieve this? He faces each topic as if it were an imaginary rug and lifts it up repeatedly—every time at a different point—which presents him with astounding variations of the original weave of his topic. In an unpublished letter to Felix Philipp Ingold, written May 22, 1984, Flusser hones in on this method: "I think writing is: to grab one single idea and let it lay as many eggs as possible before death arrives. Variations on a theme." Indeed, Flusser's goal comprises researching a poetic truth, not finding some ultimate concordance between concept and topic. Flusser's style thus remains open for all conceivable interpretations—and this applies to his written texts as well as to the presentations and lectures—and it enables continuous restructuring, additions, and abridgment, resulting in a kind of dynamic encyclopedia à la

Wikipedia, an Internet avant la lettre. Gabriel Borba's description suggests a style of thinking that provokes more thinking.

The concept of fiction is absolutely central for an understanding of Flusser's works as it extends beyond a particular literary sense. The specific meaning of the word for Flusser's thought probably gains substantially from a comparison with Jorge Luis Borges. There are reports that Borges advised his students in his lectures on literature against consulting secondary literature and criticism for the texts under discussion. Once he had them convinced, he suddenly suggested that they read all criticism and commentary of the primary literature. The students were flummoxed and did not know how to negotiate these two completely opposing recommendations. Borges's solution, however, was exceedingly simple: read the different texts as if they are different people. Proceed during the first reading as if you are a wholly naive reader; banish your critical demeanor so that you may be enraptured by the plot. During your second reading, however, act like the expert and analyze critically not only the book but especially your first reading experience. Borges insisted on the "as if" because he knew that a student of literature could be neither entirely naive nor an expert. Consequently, he defended the necessity to enforce either this or that approach to reading and to at least discuss two opposing perspectives without immediately arriving at a concluding interpretation of the text.

Flusser suggests an analogous treatment of literary works. In his essay "Waiting for Kafka," he writes,

> A literary work is the expression of an intellect. It is the linguistic form an intellect takes. Through this realization, an intellect participates in a general discussion. Thus, a literary work participates in the great conversation that we—roughly put—call "civilization." As an essential part of this conversation, the literary work has two fundamental

aspects: it puts an end to the previous conversation and calls the next one into existence. In the first case, it is an answer; in the second a provocation. There are two fundamental possibilities in the evaluation of a literary work: we can try to understand it as an answer or approach it as a provocation. In the first case we analyze the work; in the second case, we enter into dialogue with it. Criticism is the sphere of the first attempt. . . . Speculation is the sphere of the second attempt.[8]

We can deduce two disparate positions here: criticism requires curiosity and speculation, however, it is premised on sympathy, that is, engagement. Flusser prefers the second position, but he admits that a more comprehensive understanding also calls for a critical evaluation of the various intertextual connections.

Although at specific points, he focuses on works of literary fiction, he limits himself to authors directly related to his own writing. Apart from Kafka, one should mention the Czech writer Karel Čapek, whose texts Flusser consumed as a teenager and whose influence on Flusser, as we will show later, is considerable and reaches well into his later works as well. Before we get to Flusser's fable *Vampyroteuthis infernalis,* published in German in 1987—and which very likely realizes Flusser's amphibian project of philosofiction best by bordering on several discourses—we would like to preface this discussion using a quote from an interview conducted with Florian Rötzer in Karlsruhe in 1988. Here Flusser clarifies his intentions regarding the tradition of fables:

I seek to reflect on humankind and its situation from a pre-human position. This is an old tactic that, in fact, is called a fable. . . . In the traditional fables it is the animals who are allowed to speak, but it is really the critic, disguised as an animal, who has the word. Could it be possible to take up an animal position towards ourselves and to persevere in this position, that is, to view ourselves with the eyes of an animal—not a mythical creature, but an animal as described by biology? This is what I attempted to do. (*ZG,* 42)

Of Caudates and Cephalopods

The cover image of *Vampyroteuthis infernalis*—depicting the sexual encounter between a larger female and male *Vampyroteuthis*—and about fifteen drawings in the book's appendix were created by Flusser's longtime friend Louis Bec. They amend and dialogue with the text. *Vampyroteuthis* is a rare type of animal that lives in the deepest crevices of the ocean and belongs to the class of cephalopods and the subclass of squids. When Flusser was writing his book, only three specimens of these rather small animals, no longer than ten to thirteen centimeters or four to five inches, had been sighted in the South China Sea.[9] Flusser's representation of *Vampyroteuthis* is reminiscent of Julio Cortázar's fictional treatment of the axolotl, a larval, water-based amphibian that displays the remarkable ability to regenerate limbs, organs, and even parts of the brain. Cortázar narrates the fascination of a writer who encounters the animal in a public aquarium in Paris and who seeks to fathom its otherness. His obsessive engagement with the animal leads to a reversal of roles: suddenly, he finds himself on the side of the axolotl and beholds his own former face in front of the aquarium pane. He observes how he studies himself. Cortázar's axolotl is amphibian, just like his chosen genre: his fictive story does not correspond to truth, but neither is it just a lie.

To See One's Other as an Other

Flusser treats his *Vampyroteuthis* in the same fashion as Cortázar does his axolotl. By using fiction, he is able to observe something with such intensity that all of a sudden, he finds himself study-ing his own gaze. The first sentence of *Vampyroteuthis infernalis* establishes a fundamental scientific difference and calls for a set of ethical deliberations: "A genus of over 170 species. (The genus of homines is represented by only one species, all others are extinct)" (*VA*, 9). It is a rather difficult task to examine and comprehend *Vampyroteuthis* more deeply as it eludes both the fishing nets and our networks of knowledge. The pressure in its habitat would crush us, and our air would choke it. Were we to capture it in our aquariums to study its behavior, it would most likely kill itself by gorging on its tentacles, and if it suc-ceeded in kidnapping us into its depths, our behavior would be unpredictable. However, fiction presents the means with which we can understand the barrier that divides the human and *Vampyroteuthis*. If we catch the structure of *Vampyroteuthis* in a fictional net, we may soon detect traces of our own being alongside the radical differences. Flusser writes accordingly, "We can construct a game with distorted mirrors based on which we can rediscover distortedly the basic structure of our own existence from a considerable distance. Such a decidedly 'reflective' game should allow us to gain a remote but not a 'transcendental' look at ourselves . . . from the viewpoint of the vampyroteuthis, especially since it exists on this world together with us; it is a coexistence *[Mit-Sein]*" (*VA*, 12–13).

Usually, reading fictional texts requires what we have come to call a "suspension of disbelief," that is, the conscious aban-donment of suspicion. It enables us to experience what we are reading as if it were true. Flusser stipulates an additional step: he expects that we relinquish our belief in the truth of scientific models. We can achieve the suspension of disbelief toward scien-tific theories with another type of understanding that does not aim to be objective; it seeks, rather, to listen to *Vampyroteuthis* and thereby allows us to understand ourselves as humans. In an unpublished letter from 1981 to his Brazilian friend and poet Dora Ferreira da Silva, Flusser explicates his interest in these infernal cephalopods. The point is, according to Flusser, to set up a necessary distance toward the human *conditio* so that we can create a fable capable of combining scientific precision with an intricately wrought imagination.

With this idea of fiction in mind, it is not Flusser's intent to sketch out some vampyroteuthian zoology but to capture *Vampyroteuthis*'s existential circumstances and, by default—by taking a detour, so to speak—the existential sensitivities of the human who is studying the animal. His scientific program always constitutes a fictive one as well: the fable takes up the place of reality and of the object so that a new object and a new reality may transpire. Consequently, Flusser is able to divide animals into two categories without difficulty: those who are evolving in our direction, the "incomplete humans," and those that move away from us because they have pursued a different direction, the "degenerate humans" (*VA,* 14). Mammals are incomplete humans, that is, almost humans; birds, reptiles, and mollusks, however, are degenerate humans because they substantially differ from us. The ironic turn of a taxonomy so consciously simplified consists of the realization that, ultimately, we humans always end up referring to ourselves as the referential parameter and, as a consequence, gamble away any claim to objectivity. The human who considers himself the only rational being ultimately commits an irrational act. Flusser thus recapitulates the evolution of man from an ironic perspective: "Revulsion recapitulates phylogenesis. . . . Our 'collective' unconscious is imprinted with a hierarchy of revulsion that mirrors the biological hierarchy" (*VA,* 14). In the genealogical tree, the more removed an animal is from the human, the more revulsion the human feels toward this animal. If an animal that is being crushed under our shoe is soft and slippery, we who call a skeleton and a spine our own feel disgusted, as if unwilling to remember the origins of our own life.

Vampyroteuthis is a slippery mollusk that unmistakably generates revulsion. Nonetheless, its interior structure, in the form of a spiral, is tremendously complex: the animal rotates around itself, and this tendency toward rotation is so pronounced that the body rotates to a point that the mouth devours the tail—as if the mythical Ouroboros were a real animal to be encountered at the bottom of the sea:

> The head, which merges with the foot, has caused a 90 degree rotation of the axis of symmetry. What was in front becomes below, what was the back becomes the front. Therefore, the rotation of the body proceeds in the direction opposite to what we accomplished when we became erect in order to abandon the treetops for the tundra. Our hands became free and the eyes open for the horizon. The cephalopods' sensory organs move downward. The cephalopods are our antipodes: elevated intelligent bellies, not elevated brains. Only that their brains which moved downward are more complex than ours. (VA, 19–20)

Because mollusks can be found in all seas of the world, they are of a cosmopolitan disposition. They are mostly slow or even motionless, caught in their shells or in crevices. Yet the cephalopods, to which Vampyroteuthis belongs, are quick and cruel animals. Eight to ten tentacles reach from their mouths; the tentacles look like legs, but they are insufficient for locomotion. For that reason, they have another organ for movement: they eject water and can jerkily, rocketlike, catapult themselves backward with great speed. When they feed and breathe, they cause a centripetal whirl that absorbs their environment. In short, the cephalopods are animals whose breathing and locomotion is synchronized.

Vampyroteuthis has two eyes that resemble ours in astonishing ways, but they work differently. Our eyes capture the sun rays reflected by objects, whereas theirs recapture the rays sent off by their own organs illuminating the abysmal regions of the ocean. These vision and light organs can be located in all tentacles and serve to hypnotize their victims. Sexual intercourse is complex and time consuming. These animals tend toward the monogamous and display a sense for tragedy: they fluctuate between suicide and cannibalism. Either they have intercourse or they devour each other. If they cannot feed, it can even happen that they devour their own tentacles. They participate in a game that must remain alien to us: we play out of love and are thus threatened by death; they play with death and repress love. According to Flusser, it is impossible for us to copy this model because our evolution has not advanced far enough—and here he intentionally reverses the anthropomorphist viewpoint, which successfully continues to distort our representation of nature. It is Flusser's ambition to demonstrate to us the fascinating aspects of *Vampyroteuthis* because it is, in the end, nothing but our other as an other.

Perspectives and Precipices

Vampyroteuthis is so radically different from us humans that it can survive in a milieu where we would have no chance: the floor of the ocean. Because the largest part of living beings resides in the sea, we may imagine this world as an in part densely populated, fluid paradise full of sounds, lights, and colors, as a night endlessly illuminated by multiply projected rays of light, as a dancing, gleaming, whispering garden. But because we do not reside in the sea, from our perspective, we merely perceive a hellish precipice. "We see a cold black hole filled with the rattle of teeth and jaws, threatening us with an all-crushing pressure" (*VA*, 33). Whether we describe it as a paradise or as hell, both depictions are valid, and neither truly grasps that which they represent. These perspectives are models from which we need to liberate ourselves eventually. We need to emancipate ourselves from a narrow-minded trust in models, especially from the naive and distorting model according to which reality emerges from a simple encounter of a realizing subject with an object that is to be realized. We have to assume that reality as such does exist but that it ultimately cannot be grasped directly because it emerges from a dynamic intentional and intersubjective interaction between subjects and objects. "If I feel a pain in the stomach," Flusser writes in an essay about Husserl's phenomenology, "only the pain is a concrete fact; 'I' and the 'stomach' are nothing but abstract extrapolations from that concrete fact, extrapolations explaining the concrete fact."[10]

The ocean of *Vampyroteuthis* shows us that existence consists of a fluid being-in-the-world and that the structure of the world reflects that of the organisms animating it. This does not only apply to *Vampyroteuthis* but also to humans. "Organism reflects the world and the world reflects organism. Hence it is nonsense to speak of a world in general *(in abstracto)*. 'World' is a pole of human existence. Whatever happens, happens in the human world, including vampyroteuthis. It exists only in relation to me" (*VA*, 35). We recognize in *Vampyroteuthis* an existence that is comparable to ours, an existence that permits us to take the metaphorical leap from a familiar world into another fantastic one. Metaphors generate thought because they promote doubt, amazement, and wonderment, and the culture of *Vampyroteuthis* reveals human culture; but does a squid actually have something akin to culture? If we define culture as an intentional modification of the world by subjects, we have to grant both the human and the *Vampyroteuthis* culture, but with a significant difference. For the human, the world consists of problems obstructing a path; culture, therefore, constitutes itself as an acknowledgment, a treatment, and a clearing-the-path of problems. The project of human culture comprises a progressive removal of nature. The opposite is the case for *Vampyroteuthis*. "For the vampyroteuthis objects are chunks in a stream of water tumbling towards it. It absorbs them in order to ingest them. Thus, culture to the vampyroteuthis means discriminating between digestible and indigestible chunks, that is, a critique of impressions. In other words, culture does not present a project against the world, it presents a discriminating-critical injection of the world into the interior of the subject" (*VA*, 36–37).

The world of phenomena surrounding us appears to send out rays, but in reality, the objects reflect the rays of the sun. Because appearances deceive us, we believe to have to be in search of that which hides behind them. The world of *Vampyroteuthis* is an endless, dark, impenetrable night. For this reason, it needs to send out rays of light by itself so that oncoming objects become visible. "Such a world," according to Flusser, "cannot deceive as it is a self-produced appearance" (*VA*, 37). We could describe our naive position vis-à-vis appearances in Platonic terms, while that of *Vampyroteuthis,* in turn, would be a Kantian position. Our basic perspective can only be that of methodical doubt because we define ourselves primarily in opposition to the world; for *Vampyroteuthis,* which illuminates its environment to devour it, however, the basic perspective can only be that of Aristotelian amazement: "Its philosophical gaze is not contemplative but orgiastic: not philosophical tranquility, but philosophical delirium" (*VA*, 39). Flusser's gaze, then, turns the human and the *Vampyroteuthis* into equivalent philosophers; each grasps its world in its own way. His philosophical fable refers to scientific research, but only to design a kind of fictive science: he decides in favor of the simulacrum and the improbable instead of destroying one and taming the other. While he thus keeps at a distance from the scientist and approaches the poet, he remains, nonetheless, within the scientific territory. Knowledge joins subjective experience, but it does not join an outer world that is independent of a realizing subject. As a result, the true problem of philosophy no longer consists of differentiating between reality and illusion, simulacra and virtual reality.

The human and the *Vampyroteuthis* are not complementary; they are opposite each other, like mirrors. "Mirrors reflecting each other—is that not the intent of each and every fable?" (*VA*, 63). It is necessary to narrate fairy tales that force us to look into this kind of mirror. Flusser's fable seeks to overcome scientific objectivity and serves as a kind of wisdom full of illusions and secrets: the knowledge of human fate.

Intelligent Newts

A comparison between Flusser's story of *Vampyroteuthis* and Cortázar's axolotl is obligatory, but another comparison imposes itself, namely, Karel Čapek's novel *The War of the Newts*, published in 1936, at a time when the young Flusser still lived in Prague. The book tells the story of the encounter between humans and intelligent, amphibian beings who are capable of using machines and speaking several languages. Rather than reacting with astonishment and shock to this incredible discovery, humanity decides to enslave the newt. Just like Flusser after him, Čapek tries to enter the perspective of the newts, as apparent from the author's commentary on the text: "It was necessary to slip into the skin of the newts, even if only with the ultimate goal to speak about human problems. It was a rather cold and wet experience, but, after all, just as wonderful and horrific as if I had to put myself in the position of a human."[11] The fictive does not so much get applied here as a means for explanation and for the entertainment of the reader, but as a possibility to experience the way of living of a completely different being.

The way the newts are treated following the encounter

between them and the humans anticipates the inhuman and murderous practices in concentration camps that were not far off into the future and where Čapek's brother Josef and Flusser's own family were killed. When the company that studies the life of the newts decides to sell them en masse, one of the partners hypocritically demands that this needs to happen respectfully, and especially without offending human sensitivities, as if the sale of intelligent beings did not present an unscrupulous act of violence by itself. The best contemporary scientists conduct the most cruel tests on the pacifist giant newt Andreas Scheuchzeri Tschudi to measure his resistance to changes in the environment and his practical usability: the newts "exhibit considerable sensitivity to chemical factors: in experiments with greatly diluted alkali, industrial effluent, tanning agents, etc., their skin peeled off in strips and the experimental animal dies of some kind of gangrene of the gills."[12] The cynicism reaches its apex when the newt Hans, one of the best laboratory assistants, is "released" to serve as experimental food. He "was an educated and clever animal with a special talent for scientific work; it used to be employed in Dr. Hinkel's department as his laboratory assistant and it could be trusted with the most exacting chemical analyses. We used to have long chats with it in the evenings, amused by its insatiable thirst for knowledge. We were sorry to lose our Hans, but he had lost his sight in the course of my trepanation experiments. His meat was dark and spongy but there were no unpleasant after-effects."[13]

A contemporary newspaper survey inquires whether newts have a soul. George Bernhard Shaw responds succinctly: "They definitely do not have a soul. Here they correspond to the human." Shaw is being called on as a witness to demonstrate that the novel does speak of newts, of course, but very much focuses on the human, just like Flusser in his *Vampyroteuthis infernalis*. The final irony of the book is that the newts who multiplied in the depths of the oceans and who successfully copied all knowledge from humans would soon demand additional territory and ultimately declare war on humanity. Heavily armed, and with organized armies, they conduct such a war victoriously by applying the methods of the humans. Shortly thereafter, however, the newts face among themselves a murderous civil war, resulting in their complete destruction.

Flusser, in closing, comprehends the world as a gigantic ensemble of fictions; however, this is not to imply that, to him, something like reality does not exist. His idea of fiction does not correlate to lies and, as such, is not diametrically opposed to truth. He requires that we confront the fictional character of our own existence and that of the world as a whole; as a consequence, we understand fiction not simply as an aesthetic phenomenon but also as a basis for science and ethics.

7 | On Creativity: Blue Dogs with Red Spots and Dialogic Imagination

In one of his pivotal essays, "Exile and Creativity," Flusser proposes to view "exile as a challenge to creativity":

> Here is the hypothesis I propose. The expellee has been torn out of his accustomed surroundings, or has torn himself out of them. Custom and habit are a blanket that covers over reality as it exists. In our accustomed surroundings we only notice change, not what remains constant. Only change conveys information to a person who inhabits a dwelling; the permanent fixtures of his life are redundant. But in exile everything is unusual. Exile is an ocean of chaotic information. . . . Because exile is extraordinary, it is uninhabitable. In order to be able to live there, the expellee must first transform the information swirling about him into meaningful messages, that is, he must process the data. This is a matter of life and death. If he is not able to process the data, he will be swamped and consumed by the waves of exile breaking over him. Data processing is synonymous with creation. If he is not to perish the expellee must be creative. (*FM*, 81)

Flusser compares his particular aesthetic, that is, how we perceive and digest the world around us, to a blanket, which he describes in greater detail later:

> Habit is like a fluffy blanket. It rounds off all corners and damps all noise. It is unaesthetic (from *aisthestai,* perceive) because it prevents us from perceiving information such as corners or noises. Habit is felt as pleasant because it screens out perceptions, and because it anesthetizes. . . . Discovery begins as soon as the blanket is pulled away. Everything is then seen as unusual, monstrous, and "un-settling" in the true sense of the word. To understand this one merely has to consider one's own right hand and finger movements from the point of view of, say, a Martian. It becomes an octopus-like monstrosity. (*FM,* 82–83)

At this point of the expellee discovering that he or she must be creative and the in-habit-ant realizing that his hand might be anything but familiar and is therefore exiled from his body, according to Flusser, dialogue becomes possible, and we can become creative:

> At the outset I stated that creating is synonymous with data processing. What I meant was that the creation of new information depends on the synthesis of prior information. Such a synthesis consists in an exchange of information, and storing this information in individual memory or various memories. One can therefore speak of creation as a dialogical process, in which either an internal or external dialog takes place. . . . When such internal and external dialogs resonate with each other, not only the world, but the settled inhabitants and expellees as well are transformed creatively. That is what I meant when I said that the freedom of the expellee

consists in remaining foreign, different from the others. It is the freedom to change oneself and others. (*FM*, 86)

Creativity, arguably Flusser's most central philosophical concept, lies at the basis of all communication, dialogue, and life because the aesthetic experience lies at the center of human perception.

Dialogism in Art

The dialogic principle within the realm of critical theory invokes, first and foremost, Mikhail Bakhtin's heteroglossic approach to literature and philosophy, specifically his theory of the novel. It hints at Martin Buber's 1923 *I and Thou*, published in 1937, and is echoed in Bakhtin's early essay titled "Art and Answerability" (although dialogism marks the entirety of Bakhtin's oeuvre). According to Eduardo Kac, who credits Flusser with being one initiator—if not *the* initiator—of biogenetic art, it refers in the visual arts to "interrelationship and connectivity" in "dialogic artworks": "The dialogic principle changes our conception of art; it offers a new way of thinking that requires the use of bidirectional or multidirectional media and the creation of situations that can actually promote intersubjective experiences that engage two or more individuals in real dialogic exchanges . . . that I call 'multilogic interactions.'"[1]

The ubiquity of the term and its approximate equivalents— *dialogicity, polyphony, intersubjectivity, connectivity*—signify a shift in Western aesthetic, philosophical, sociopolitical, and ethical stances that helped bring about new fields, including postcolonialism. As Jeffrey T. Nealon points out, "dialogic intersubjectivity, understood in terms of an impassioned play of voices, has displaced the dominant modernist and existentialist metaphor of the monadic subject and its plaintive demand for social recognition and submission from the other."[2] This play of voices comes to bear not only on the ideaness of the total artwork but also on the critiques and discussions the idea as art proposition have launched—as a dialogic entity, it inevitably invites dialogue and exchange.

Bakhtinian dialogism, as defined by Michael Holquist, gains in importance, too, at this point inasmuch as the center (of the artist, of the self, of the artwork, of the community) also loses prominence: "In dialogism consciousness is otherness. More accurately, it is the differential relation between a center and all that is not the center."[3] The monadic subject finds its end, things fall apart, and the center loses itself. All is relative? Well, not precisely, because both phenomenology and Bakhtin's philosophy teach us to take the "object" as something "other" to which we, too, are "other" and with which we engage mutually.

One such dialogue—an example of "multilogic interaction"—is played out in the fable authored by Flusser and the interrelated bio art by the French artist and self-described zoosystematician Louis Bec. *Vampyroteuthis infernalis* (the "vampire squid from hell," as Eduardo Kac called it), already under discussion in chapter 6, juxtaposes humans and a type of giant octopus to answer some fundamental questions about dialogic intersubjectivity in light of humans' anthropocentric positionality.[4] Flusser's guiding question, as related in a 1988 interview with Florian Rötzer, focuses on the issue of otherness: "Would it be possible to position oneself as an animal vis-à-vis humans and to remain within that position, that is, to see us with the eyes of an animal?" (ZG, 45). He chose the octopus because the cephalopod has a nervous system that is proximate to that of humans, among other similarities, and he collaborated with Louis Bec on a synthesis of languaging and imaging this animal, which, despite its verisimilitude to nature, remained a literary and visual projection for both. According to Flusser, their bridging words and images yielded stunning results that went against the negative dialectics of the mutual exclusion or erasure of the two art forms, the literary and the visual:

> In this collaboration with Louis Bec we created an unexpected synthesis because my texts do not explain Bec's images and his images do not illustrate my texts, but, rather, the brute, the octopus, indeed only came into being as a result of this synthesis of Bec's images and my texts.... This is a new way to philosophize. The new thing is not the brute, and neither is it the method; it is the experience of a possible collaboration between discursive and imaginary reason, from which emerges something new.[5]

Intersubjective dialogue and multilogic interaction take place on two levels here: *within* the book, the *Vampyroteuthis infernalis* positioned as an othering of humans, and *without* the book, between two collaborators who move beyond their individual arts, the textual and the visual, but not to describe the images away via language or to undermine the text by covering it or expressing it with an image; rather, the two artistic modes complement each other to such a degree so that what is to be presented can only find creation through both arts together. In a way, it constitutes either a process of birthing, of course, or the aesthetic expression of a Hegelian synthesis, but Bec has, in fact, created a plethora of images of types of octopuses that also turn up in different media. The images shown on the *Flusser Studies* Web site are digital, but a 2007 retrospective of Bec's work in Prague showed entirely fictitious genealogies of cephalopods and their various imagined biological data on the kind of hanging maps formerly in use in chemistry, physics, and biology classes. They were worked in relief, with elements hanging down and sticking out, hinting at an unfinished three-dimensionality. The exhibition served, for Bec, as a means of continuing "our interrupted dialogue," broken off by Flusser's untimely death in 1991.[6] In that sense, the fictitious world of the animal, brought about by conjoining two artistic expressions and different media to confront, fundamentally, the fictitiousness of humans' spatiality and virtuality—or as Bec would put it, their parallel zoologies—is itself complemented by the unfinalizability of the artists' dialogue with each other, with their creature, and with their audiences.[7]

The Making of Art

In one of the last essays published before his death in 1991, Flusser defined the making of art as follows:

> When making art, the task is . . . to produce something that does not yet exist, that is, something that could not be anticipated by any program. We should not look at the *work of art* as a *plant* that was developed and unfurled from some randomly available seed, but as a *seed* from which something shall develop and unfurl in its recipients, a new experience with new realizations and values, for example. The artist, after all, wants to be someone who produces seeds or works out programs, not someone who scatters seeds and watches over their growth. . . . Yet, because current usage calls such a noble artist, such a producer of *logoi spermatikoi,* an *author,* we have to object. The original meaning of *auctor* is not the issue here; at issue is the fact that we are dealing with a myth, which obfuscates the making of art as it occurs today. The talk about the author stands in the way of a disciplined and self-confident making of art. Indeed, authors should not be present in the territory of art![8]

Though Flusser certainly does not sum up his complex understanding of art or art making in this short passage, he calls attention to the idea of the artist as producer and to the work of art as that which marks the beginning of something. The artist does not watch over or manage the growth—she simply makes a beginning possible, and according to Flusser, she should thereafter fade into the background. His argument appears as a thoroughly Barthesian move to cut off the author–artist from the work and to let the work of art flourish in whichever direction or dimension it pleases, tended and formed by its recipients, away and dislodged from its origins. Flusser, however, seeks to call attention to something else as well: by writing about a generic "making of art," he is trying to attack a stubborn cultural position on "two cultures" whereby the artificial separation of science and art or humanities should be abandoned in the interest of a much more multimodal and interdisciplinary approach to creativity, ideas, the making of experiences, and the production of knowledge.

Significantly, in an interview for the Brazilian journal *Superinteressante,* published in 1986, Flusser urged art and science to agree on a common language:

> It makes no sense today to query one of the synthetic, computer-generated images or fractals whether they are art or science. If they are art, then they are a very exact art. It makes no sense to find out whether these images were created by artists or by scientists. If, indeed, they were created by scientists, then they are very beautiful artworks, and if they were created by artists, then they are extraordinarily accurate conceptual compositions. There is no difference any more between art and science. (ZG, 31)

In the following, then, we continue to put forth a reading of Flusserian aesthetics as creativity emerging from exile as it is linked to digital aesthetics, speculative computing, ideas, and their realizations (or not) in art; to experience and aisthesis; or to creativity in general in the in-between territories of interdisciplinary inquiry and unfamiliar territory. For some of the artistic practices Flusser conjured up in the 1980s are only now finding expression in, for example, bioart or transgenic art—most importantly, perhaps, Eduardo Kac's *GFP Bunny*.[9] Lev Manovich's cultural analytics projects provide other examples, most fittingly for this context, his "Interactive Visualization of Image Collections for Humanities Research," which exhibits how Mark Rothko's paintings became data to be graphed into paintings that documented "patterns and trends in a painter's life."[10] Though some of Manovich's work within cultural analytics remains questionable,[11] his explorations surely echo Flusser's ideas and questions during the 1980s.

However, if we search for something akin to a Flusserian concept of art history or theory, we come up (relatively) empty. In an unpublished article, Rainer Guldin probes one of Flusser's essays on the topic, "L'art: le beau et le joli," part of his *Les Phénomènes de la Communication* (1975–76), and concludes that Flusser's idea of art and art making is based on poeietic principles: it creates reality, it is closely linked to everyday life, it has the power to bestow meaning to our being-in-the-world, and it allows us to design models with which we communicate and create new worlds. According to Flusser, "art is that aspect of communication which broadens information as it relates to concrete experience. . . . We need art to be able to perceive the world."[12] In fact, concrete experience has the potential to become projected experience and to turn each individual into a potential artist, the creator of alternative worlds: art is creativity linked to design, resulting in unknown possibilities. In that sense, Flusser's conception of art and creativity contains an activist and forward-looking element as well, as apparent in his essay on "The Photograph as Post-industrial Object":

Ever since the fifteenth century, Occidental civilization has suffered from the divorce into two cultures: science and its techniques—the "true" and the "good for something"—on the one hand; the arts—beauty—on the other. This is a pernicious distinction. Every scientific proposition and every technical gadget has an aesthetic quality, just as every work of art has an epistemological and political quality. More significantly, there is no basic distinction between scientific and artistic research: both are fictions in the quest of truth (scientific hypotheses being fictions).

Electromagnetized images do away with this divorce because they are the result of science and are at the service of the imagination. They are what Leonardo da Vinci used to call "fantasia essata." A synthetic image of a fractal equation is both a work of art and a model for knowledge. Thus the new photo not only does away with the traditional classification of the various arts (it is painting, music, literature, dance and theatre all rolled into one), but it also does away with the distinction between the "two cultures" (it is both art and science).[13]

Flusser explored such antidisciplinary approaches to creativity repeatedly, and the topic travels through a number of his texts.[14] The 1980s, in particular, mark the period during which Flusser aggressively investigated what he observed as diminishing differences between art and science in some depth, at least judging from his prolific output beginning with *Für eine Philosophie der Fotographie* (1983), *Ins Universum der technischen Bilder* (1984), *Vampyroteuthis infernalis* (1987), and, finally, *Die Schrift: Hat Schreiben Zukunft?* (1987). All these texts, including others as well, address his specific understanding of creativity, art, aesthetics, or aisthesis and, in particular, his theory of the image and the technical image. Yet this approach to creating and dialoguing in everyday contexts was received in Europe—where Flusser soon verged on being viewed a prophet, albeit a critical one, of virtual reality—as media theory and philosophy of communication, whereas his engagement in Brazil, where he had been an active participant in artistic circles since the early 1970s, was no longer taken into consideration. It may well be for that reason that he turned to a third continent, specifically the United States, to explore the collapse of art and science into each other further; there he found a welcoming venue for his ideas on art, science, and everyday creative dialogue.

Flusser at *artforum*

According to Sarah Thornton, who refers to *artforum international* simply as "The Magazine," the periodical "is to art what *Vogue* is to fashion and *Rolling Stone* was to rock and roll. It's a trade magazine with crossover cachet and an institution with controversial clout."[15] Founded in 1962 in California, *artforum,* after a move to New York in the 1960s and an editorial dispute in the 1970s (which ended in the creation of another well-known journal of art criticism, *October*), established itself as an international platform for contemporary art. In 1980, Ingrid Sischy, herself an artist, was appointed editor and, as the critic Jerry Saltz has observed, made the magazine hip: "She had a great sense of timing which saved the magazine from ever being inextricably linked to any one set of artists, or too intent on seeing the success of any one movement. No—'Artforum' just wanted to be where the action was and maybe lead the pack—and it did. The January 1980 issue of 'Artforum' had 94 pages—by the end of 1989 it had increased to 180 pages."[16]

Flusser's first piece in *artforum* was published in the September 1986 issue, titled "Curies' Children: Vilem *[sic]* Flusser on Science." In a letter dated June 8 of the same year, the managing editor, Kathryn Howard, referred to a conversation with Flusser in which they discussed the publication of "Taking Leave of Literature." He would be paid three hundred dollars on publication or a one hundred dollar kill fee should it remain unpublished. Howard familiarizes Flusser with their editorial procedures, and the following letters point to a close relationship with the managing editor (Charles V. Miller as of September 1986), who encouraged, but on occasion also disciplined, the overly productive columnist Flusser.[17] In fact, though Flusser provided specific titles for his pieces, *artforum* decided to print more generic names of Flusser's texts, fitting the columnist's genre.

While all twenty columns echo the texts produced in other languages and for other venues, Flusser clearly explores the limits of a territory or territories that mark even an adventurous contemporary art magazine. Unsurprisingly, he commences his first text from September 1986 with a bang, mirroring the essay in *Leonardo*: "We are about to enter the age of electromagnetism. Microelectronics, artificial intelligence, robotics, and holography are some of the signposts on our path away from a material culture and toward an 'immaterial' one in which we will concentrate on the processing of rays rather than on the manipulation of inert, perfidious matter." He concludes, after weaving together a web involving reason, modernity, light, and the juxtaposition of mental and material energy, that "this is the metaphor that suggests itself to identify this new age: there is an ocean of light, which is partly visible and partly not, and all things are permeated by it. So are we ourselves; our reason is one means by which this ocean of light infuses us. In fact, everything about us, our own bodies, our own minds, are soaked with radiation."

From here on, Eduardo Kac's radiated bunny is not a farfetched contraption or hallucination of modern science or artistic imagination. Pointedly, Flusser continues to develop his notion of science, art, thinking, and creating as one and the same in his work for *artforum,* and his columns soon receive the subtitle "Vilém Flusser on Discovery." In his March 1988 column, he begins his exploration of biotechnics: "The word seems a Greek-derived version of the Latin *ars vivendi,* but it is quite different in climate from the ancient sense of the term. In fact, it is a discipline out of which a whole world of artificial living beings—living artworks—will arise." In the October issue of the same year, Flusser proposes bolder steps: "Why is it that dogs aren't yet blue with red spots, and that horses don't yet radiate phosphorescent colors over the nocturnal meadows of the land? Why hasn't the breeding of animals, still principally an economic concern, moved into the field of esthetics?" Indeed, "why can't art inform nature? When we ask why dogs can't be blue with red spots, we're really asking about art's role in the immediate future, which is menaced not only by explosions both nuclear and demographic, but equally by the explosion of boredom."

Flusser here applies the shifting structures of his philosophical thinking—on doubt, on media, on communication, on culture—to the parameters, such as they are, of art and poses questions that might be familiar at this point in our introduction. Similarly, he questions not only epistemological formations and encrustations in art making but also those of architecture (e.g., columns published in 1990) and of the environment. Indeed, he published a column on popes in the 1990 October issue, significantly a critique of art criticism, continuing with the trope of trinities in subsequent columns in which he writes about "Three Times" (February 1991) and "Three Spaces" (May 1991). Ironically, in his next to last column, published in the November 1991 issue, in the month of his death, Flusser focuses on books, predicting the loss of letters in the image flood of the new digital age, wondering whether "the majestic river of letters passed down to us through Homer, Dante, and Shakespeare . . . stagnate into a muddy, swampy delta?" We have yet to find out. For Flusser, the "space" in *artforum* presented a stimulating opportunity to try out his ideas and texts from elsewhere with another audience and in another language, and we can only assume that *artforum* would have kept him on as a columnist into the 1990s.

We would like to close with a quote by Johanna Drucker, who, akin to Flusser's idea of art making and creativity, summarized the coincidence of art and digital culture by referring to conceptual art of the 1960s:

> The conceptual artists of the 1960s struggled to dematerialize art. In the process they made us aware of a very fundamental principle of art making—the distinction between the idea of algorithmic procedure that instigates a work and the manifestation or execution of a specific iteration. . . . Every iteration of a digital work is inscribed in the memory trace of the computational system in a highly explicit expression. Aesthetics is a property of experience and knowledge provoked by works structured or situated to maximize that provocation. The mediated character of experience becomes intensified in digital work.[18]

Metaphorically speaking, it is at this moment of mediation and intensification that the foreigner, the other, engages in productive dialogue with the in-habit-ant, also an other, a moment when creativity becomes possible and when Flusser, despite doubts and hesitations, sees the potential for a new creativity realized—most significantly, his call for "A New Imagination" (*Eine neue Einbildungskraft*) and his faith in humans capable of entirely poietic imagery in a digital age.[19] This is also what his very last book, *From Subject to Project: Becoming Human,* was about.

Notes

Introduction

1   Flusser, "Mein Atlas," in *Dinge und Undinge*, 113–17. Unless otherwise noted, all translations are by Anke Finger.

2   Flusser, *Writings*; Flusser, *Freedom of the Migrant*; Flusser, *Shape of Things*.

3   Susanne Klengel and Holger Siever, eds., *Das Dritte Ufer: Vilém Flusser und Brasilien* (Würzburg, Germany: Königshausen and Neumann, 2009).

4   Flusser, *Língua e realidade*.

5   Flusser, *A história do diabo*. Also available in German as *Die Geschichte des Teufels* (Göttingen, Germany: European Photography, 2006).

6   Flusser, *Pós-História*. Also available in German as *Nachgeschichte: Eine korrigierte Geschichtsschreibung* (Frankfurt, Germany: Fischer, 1997).

7   Flusser, *Toward a Philosophy of Photography*. Available in numerous languages, including German, French, Portuguese, Dutch, Spanish, and Czech.

8   Flusser, *Into the Universe of Technical Images*.

9   Flusser, *Does Writing Have a Future?*

10   Flusser and Bec, *Vampyroteuthis infernalis*.

11   Flusser, *Angenommen*.

12   Flusser, *Gesten*. Also available in French and Spanish.

13   Flusser, *Bodenlos*. Also available in Portuguese and Czech.

14   Flusser, *Shape of Things*.

15   Flusser, *Brasilien oder die Suche nach dem neuen Menschen*. Also available in Portuguese as *Fenomenologia do brasileiro: em busca de um novo homem* (Rio de Janeiro, Brazil: EDUERJ, 1998).

16   Flusser, *Jude sein*.

17   Flusser, *Vom Subjekt zum Projekt*.

18   Flusser, *Kommunikologie*.

19   Dermot Moran, *Edmund Husserl: Founder of Phenomenology* (London: Polity Press, 2007), and David Woodruff Smith, *Husserl* (New York: Routledge, 2006).

20   Matthew Calarco, *Zoographies: The Question of the Animal from Heidegger to Derrida* (New York: Columbia University Press, 2008), 10.

21   Kelly Oliver, *Animal Lessons: How They Teach Us to Be Human* (New York: Columbia University Press, 2009).

22   Katherine Hayles, *How We Became Posthuman: Virtual Bodies in Cybernetics, Literature, and Informatics* (Chicago: University of Chicago Press, 1999). See also Cary Wolfe, *What Is Posthumanism?* (Minneapolis: University of Minnesota Press, 2009).

23   Flusser, *Freedom of the Migrant*, 3–4.

24   Ibid., 14.

25   Don Ihde, *Expanding Hermeneutics: Visualism in Science* (Evanston, IL: Northwestern University Press, 1998).

1. Migration, Nomadism, Networks

1   The first part of the interview with Edith Flusser, from which we draw here, was published in *Flusser Studies* 05 (2007), http://www.flusserstudies.net/pag/05/Interview.pdf, and is based on long conversations with Anke Finger in 2007. This kind of oral history does not aspire to critical scholarship and always

contains ambiguities, as emphasized by scholars of memory studies such as Aleida Assmann. In 2007, Edith Flusser was eighty-seven years old. She recounted her life reluctantly, but her youthful spirit and considerable memory bring forth stories, people, and events that have heretofore been unknown to the public; as such, these stories, people, and events provide initial information on her and Vilém Flusser's lives until additional research becomes available. Nonetheless, and as Aleida Assmann has pointed out by referring to Margaret Atwood, the person who experienced the events and encountered the people described has not remained and could not have remained the same. Aleida Assmann, *Einführung in die Kulturwissenschaft: Grundbegriffe, Themen, Fragestellungen* (Berlin: Erich Schmidt, 2006), 183.

2   Rainer Guldin, *Philosophieren zwischen den Sprachen: Vilém Flussers Werk* (Munich, Germany: Wilhelm Fink, 2006), 14.

3   Vilém Flusser, "The City as Wave-Trough in the Image-Flood," *Critical Inquiry* (Winter 2005): 324–25.

4   Peter Demetz, *Prague in Black and Gold: The History of a City* (London: Penguin Books, 1997), 339.

5   For more information on Flusser's father, consult the thorough investigation of Ines Koeltzsch, "Gustav Flusser: Biographische Spuren eines deutschen Juden in Prag vor dem Zweiten Weltkrieg," *Flusser Studies* 05 (2007), http://www.flusserstudies.net/pag/05/Gustav-Flusser.pdf.

6   Edith Flusser, "Prager Erinnerungen," *Flusser Studies* 05 (2007), http://www.flusserstudies.net/pag/05/Interview.pdf.

7   Ibid., 10.

8   Ibid., 11–12.

9   Ibid., 11–12.

10   Ibid., 13.

11   Ibid., 16.

12   Ibid., 19.

13   Flusser, *Writings,* 194.

14   Ibid., 207.

15   Silvia Wagnermaier and Nils Röller, eds., *Absolute Vilém Flusser*

(Freiburg, Germany: Orange Press, 2003), 111.

16 Ibid., 119.

3. Translation and Multilingual Writing

1 This text is available in German, translated by Edith Flusser, in Rainer Guldin, ed., *Das Spiel mit der Übersetzung: Figuren der Mehrsprachigkeit in Vilém Flussers Werk* (Tübingen, Germany: Francke, 2004), 15–46.

2 For a discussion of the cultural turn in German-speaking translation studies, see Doris Bachmann-Medick, *Cultural Turns: Neuorientierungen in den Kulturwissenschaften* (Hamburg, Germany: Rororo, 2009).

3 Vilém Flusser, "Thought and Reflection," *Flusser Studies* 01 (2005): 3, http://www.flusserstudies.net/pag/01/thought-reflection01.pdf.

4 See Norval Baitello, *Flussers Völlerei* (Cologne, Germany: Walther König, 2007).

5 Vilém Flusser, "Retradução enquanto método de trabalho," unpublished typescript, 4. Translated from Portuguese by Rainer Guldin.

6 Wolfgang Iser, "Coda to the Discussion," in *The Translatability of Cultures: Figurations of the Space Between,* ed. Sanford Budick and Wolfgang Iser (Palo Alto, Calif.: Stanford University Press, 1996), 301.

7 Ibid.

8 Flusser, "Retradução," 2.

9 Iser, "Coda," 301.

10 Bachmann-Medick, *Cultural Turns,* 242.

11 Vilém Flusser, "In Search of Meaning," in *Writings,* 206.

12 Vilém Flusser, "The Gesture of Writing," unpublished typescript.

13 Vilém Flusser, "Barroco Mineiro visto de Praga," *Jornal do Commercio,* April 3, 1966.

14　Bachmann-Medick, *Cultural Turns,* 245.

15　Lawrence Venuti, *The Translator's Invisibility: A History of Translation* (London: Routledge, 1995).

4. Cultural Studies and Phenomenology

1　Andreas Ströhl, *Writings* (Minneapolis: University of Minnesota Press, 2002), 198.

2　Ibid., 198–99.

3　Lawrence Grossberg, "Does Cultural Studies Have Futures? Should It? (Or What's the Matter with New York? Cultural Studies, Contexts, and Conjunctures," *Cultural Studies* 20, no. 1 (2006): 1–32. See also Lawrence Grossberg, Cary Nelson, and Paula Treichler, eds., *Cultural Studies* (New York: Routledge, 1991).

4　Chris Barker, *Cultural Studies: Theory and Practice* (London: Sage, 2003), 436–37.

5　Vilém Flusser, *Bochumer Vorlesungen 1991,* ed. Silvia Wagnermaier and Siegfried Zielinski, programmed by David Link, 2005, http://www.flusser-archive.org/publications/bochumervorlesungen/.

6　Walter Mignolo, *Local Histories/Global Designs: Coloniality, Subaltern Knowledges, and Border Thinking* (Princeton, N.J.: Princeton University Press, 2000), 265.

7　Rainer Guldin, *Philosophieren zwischen den Sprachen: Vilém Flussers Werk* (Munich, Germany: Wilhelm Fink, 2003), 12.

8　Emily Apter, *The Translation Zone: A New Comparative Literature* (Princeton, N.J.: Princeton University Press, 2006), 11.

9　Vilém Flusser, "Nomaden," in *Herbstbuch eins: auf und davon: Eine Nomadologie der Neunziger,* ed. Gerhard Haberl (Graz, Austria: Verlag Droschl, 1990), 68.

10　Ströhl, *Writings,* 43–44.

11　Barker, *Cultural Studies,* 436.

12　Bill Brown, ed., *Things* (Chicago: Chicago University Press, 2004), 6. See also Arjun Appadurai, ed., *The Social Life of Things:*

Commodities in Cultural Perspective (Cambridge: Cambridge University Press, 1988).

13 Ibid., 7.

14 Vilém Flusser, "On Edmund Husserl," *Review of the Society for the History of Czechoslovak Jews* 1 (1987): 98.

15 Ibid., 98–99.

16 David Woodruff Smith, *Husserl* (New York: Routledge, 2007), 7.

17 Homi K. Bhabha, *The Location of Culture* (New York: Routledge, 1994), 163.

18 Ibid., 145.

19 Vilém Flusser, "Glaubensverlust," in *Lob der Oberflächlichkeit* (Bensheim, Germany: Bollmann, 1993), 72.

20 Ibid., 74.

21 Vilém Flusser, "Ästhetische Erziehung," in *Schöne Aussichten? Ästhetische Bildung in einer technisch-medialen Welt,* ed. Wolfgang Zacharias (Essen, Germany: Klartext, 1991), 124.

5. Communication and Media Theory

1 Flusser, *Writings,* 31.

2 Andrew E. Benjamin, *Translation and the Nature of Philosophy: A Theory of New Words* (New York: Routledge, 1989), 98.

3 Ibid., 101–2.

6. Science as Fiction, Fiction as Science

1 Cited in Brento Prado Jr., "A chuva universal de Flusser," *Folha de São Paulo,* February 13, 1999.

2 Vilém Flusser, "Da ficção," *O Diário,* August 26, 1966.

3 Friedrich Nietzsche, "On Truth and Lie in an Extra-moral Sense," in *The Viking Portable Nietzsche,* trans. Walter Kaufmann (New York: Penguin Books, 1977), 46–47.

4 Hans Vaihinger, *The Philosophy of "As If": A System of Theoretical,*

Practical, and Religious Fictions of Mankind (New York: Harcourt, Brace, 1925), 81–84.

5   Vilém Flusser, "Do espelho," *O Estado de São Paulo,* August 6, 1966.

6   Abraham Moles, "Philosophiefiktionen bei Vilém Flusser," in *Überflusser,* ed. Volker Rapsch (Düsseldorf, Germany: Bollmann, 1990), 61.

7   See Borba Filho, "Presença de Flusser," in *Vilém Flusser no Brasil,* ed. Gustavo Bernardo Krause and Ricardo Mendes (Rio de Janeiro, Brazil: AnnaBlume, 2000), 34.

8   Flusser, *Writings,* 150.

9   See also a National Geographic video on this animal, "The Vampire from the Abyss," http://www.youtube.com/watch?v=l3PvvT_Ktx8.

10 Vilém Flusser, "On Edmund Husserl," *Review of the Society for the History of Czechoslovak Jews* 1 (1987): 95.

11 Karel Čapek, *A Guerra das salamandas* (Lisbon: Editorial Caminho, 1979), 253. Translated by Rainer Guldin.

12 Karel Čapek, *War with the Newts* (Highland Park, N.J.: Catbird Press, 1985), 139.

13 Ibid., 140.

7. On Creativity

1   Eduardo Kac, "Negotiating Meaning: The Dialogic Imagination in Electronic Art," in *Bakhtinian Perspectives on Language and Culture: Meaning in Languages Art and New Media,* ed. Finn Bostad and Craig Brandist, 199–216 (New York: Palgrave Macmillan, 2004). See also Kac, ed., *Signs of Life: Bio Art and Beyond* (Cambridge, Mass.: MIT Press, 2007).

2   Jeffrey T. Nealon, *Alterity Politics: Ethics and the Performance of Subjectivity* (Durham, N.C.: Duke University Press, 1998), 33.

3   Michael Holquist, *Dialogism: Bakhtin and His World* (London: Routledge, 1990), 18.

4   Flusser and Bec, *Vampyroteuthis infernalis.*

5   Flusser, *Zwiegespräche,* 45. For examples of Bec's images, consult the following Web page: http://www.flusserstudies.net/pag/archive04.htm.

6   Louis Bec, "On *Vampyroteuthis infernalis,*" http://enter3.org/index.php?lang=en&node=110&id=67&act=detart.

7   For a lucid discussion of the philosophy of the animal, see Matthew Calarco, *Zoographies: The Question of the Animal from Heidegger to Derrida* (New York: Columbia University Press, 2008).

8   Vilém Flusser, "Vom Autor oder vom Wachsen," in *Kunst Machen? Gespräche und Essays,* ed. Florian Rötzer and Sara Rogenhofer (Munich, Germany: Boer, 1991), 58.

9   See http://www.flusserstudies.net/pag/08/2.htm.

10 See http://www.youtube.com/watch?v=-YlT1qFhJhk&feature=player_embedded.

11 See http://networkcultures.org/wpmu/query/2009/11/15/lev-manovich-studying-culture-with-search-algorithms/.

12 Cited in Rainer Guldin, "'Kunst ist poiesis': sie er-schafft die Wirklichkeit. Überlegungen zu Vilém Flussers Kunstverständnis" (unpublished manuscript, 2010), 2. For another excellent short exploration of Flusser and art, see Simone Osthoff, "Introduction," *Flusser Studies* 08 (2009), http://www.flusserstudies.net/pag/08/introduction.pdf.

13 Vilém Flusser, "The Photograph as Post-industrial Object: An Essay on the Ontological Standing of Photographs," *Leonardo* 19, no. 4 (1986): 331.

14 For readers of German, a good summary of Flusser's ideas on art is available in Florian Rötzer, *Philosophen-Gespräche zur Kunst,* 140–70 (Munich, Germany: Boer, 1991).

15 Sarah Thornton, *Seven Days in the Art World* (New York: W. W. Norton, 2008), 145.

16 Irving Sandler, *Art of the Postmodern Era* (Boulder, Colo.: Westview Press, 1996), 435–36.

17   Letter exchange between Miller and Flusser.

18   Johanna Drucker, *Speclab: Digital Aesthetics and Projects in Speculative Computing* (Chicago: University of Chicago Press, 2009), 182.

19   For a thorough discussion of Flusser's technical image, see Rainer Guldin, "Iconoclasm and Beyond: Vilém Flusser's Concept of Techno-Imagination," *Studies in Communication Sciences* 7, no. 2 (2007): 63–83.

Bibliography of Vilém Flusser's Major Texts

A história do diabo [History of the Devil]. São Paulo, Brazil: Martins, 1965.

Angenommen: eine Szenenfolge [Supposed: A Succession of Scenes]. Göttingen, Germany: European Photography, 2000.

Bodenlos: eine philosophische Autobiographie [Rootless: A Philosophical Autobiography]. Frankfurt, Germany: Fischer, 1992.

Brasilien oder die Suche nach dem neuen Menschen: Für eine Phämenologie der Unterentwicklung [Brazil or the Search for a New Human: Toward a Phenomenology of Underdevelopment]. Mannheim, Germany: Bollmann, 1994.

Da religiosidade [Of Religiosity]. São Paulo, Brazil: Conselho Estadual de Cultura, Comissão de Literatura, 1967.

Dinge und Undinge: Phänomenologische Skizzen [Things and Nonthings/ Absurdities: Phenomenological Sketches]. Munich, Germany: Hanser, 2006.

Does Writing Have a Future? Minneapolis: University of Minnesota Press, 2011.

Filosofía da caixa preta: Ensaios para uma filosofía da fotografía [Philosophy of the Black Box: Essays toward a Philosophy of Photography]. São Paulo, Brazil: Relume Dumará, 2005.

The Freedom of the Migrant: Objections to Nationalism, ed. Anke Finger, trans. Kenneth Kronenberg. Champaign: University of Illinois Press, 2003.

Gesten: Versuch einer Phänomenologie [Gestures: Attempt toward a Phenomenology]. Frankfurt, Germany: Fischer, 1997.

Into the Universe of Technical Images. Minneapolis: University of Minnesota Press, 2011.

Jude sein: Essays, Briefe, Fiktionen [Being Jewish: Essays, Letters, Fictions], ed. Stefan Bollman and Edith Flusser. Berlin: Philo, 2000.

Krise der Linearität [Crisis of Linearity]. Bern, Switzerland: Benteli, 1992.

Kommunikologie [Communicology], ed. Stefan Bollman and Edith Flusser. Frankfurt, Germany: Fischer, 1998.

Kommunikologie weiter Denken: die Bochumer Vorlesungen [Continuing to Think Communicology: The Bochum Lectures], ed. Silvia Wagnermaier. Frankfurt, Germany: Fischer, 2009.

Língua e realidade [Language and Reality]. São Paulo, Brazil: Herder, 1963.

Lob der Oberflächlichkeit: für eine Phänomenologie der Medien [In Praise of Superficiality: Toward a Phenomenology of Media]. Bensheim, Germany: Bollmann, 1993.

Medienkultur [Media Culture]. Frankfurt, Germany: Fischer, 2008.

Naturalmente: Vários acessos ao significado da natureza [Naturally: Various Essays on the Significance of Nature]. São Paulo, Brazil: Livr. Duas Cidades, 1979.

Pós-História: vinte instantâneos e um modo de usar [Posthistory: A Corrected Historiography]. São Paulo, Brazil: Livraria Duas Cidades, 1983.

The Shape of Things: A Philosophy of Design, ed. Martin Pawley, trans. Anthony Mathews. London: Reaktion Books, 1999.

Standpunkte: Texte zur Fotografie [Positionings: Texts on Photography]. Göttingen, Germany: European Photography, 1998.

Toward a Philosophy of Photography. London: Reaktion Books, 2005.

Vampyroteuthis infernalis: eine Abhandlung samt Befund des Institut Scientifique de Recherche Paranaturaliste [*Vampyroteuthis infernalis: A Treatise, Including a Report, from the Scientific Institute for Paranaturalist Research*]. Coauthored with Louis Bec. Göttingen, Germany: European Photography, 1987.

Vogelflüge: Essays zu Natur und Kultur [Bird Flights: Essays on Nature and Culture]. Munich, Germany: Hanser, 2000.

Vom Subjekt zum Projekt: Menschwerdung [From Subject to Project: On Becoming Human]. Frankfurt, Germany: Fischer, 1998.

Vom Zweifel [On Doubt]. Göttingen, Germany: European Photography, 2006.

Writings, ed. Andreas Ströhl, trans. Erik Eisel. Minneapolis: University of Minnesota Press, 2002.

Zwiegespräche: Interviews 1967–1991 [Interviews]. Göttingen, Germany: European Photography, 1996.

Index

Anke Finger is associate professor of German studies and comparative literary and cultural studies at the University of Connecticut. Among her areas of research are German and comparative modernism, aesthetics, media theory, and interart studies. Her publications include two books on the total artwork. She edited the translation of Vilém Flusser's *The Freedom of the Migrant: Objections to Nationalism,* and she cofounded and coedits (with Rainer Guldin) the online journal *Flusser Studies.*

Rainer Guldin is professor of German language and culture at the Faculty of Communication Sciences of the Università della Svizzera Italiana in Lugano, Switzerland. His numerous publications include monographs on Flusser's philosophy, the art and aesthetic history of clouds, and metaphors of the body as well as articles on Flusser, translation, British literature, and intercultural communication.

Gustavo Bernardo is professor of theory of literature at the Instituto de Letras da Universidade do Estado do Rio de Janeiro in Brazil. He has published scholarly works and fiction and is a literary scholar, especially on Machado de Assis, and a creative writer.